D0045122

BOOKS BY
RICHARD HOUGH

*The Fleet that had to Die*
*Admirals in Collision*
*Dreadnought: A History of the Modern Battleship*
*First Sea Lord: an authorised Life of Admiral Lord Fisher*
*The Blind Horn's Hate*
*Captain Bligh and Mr Christian*
*Louis and Victoria: the first Mountbattens*
*One Boy's War*
*and others*

# Advice to My Grand-daughter

LETTERS FROM QUEEN VICTORIA
TO PRINCESS VICTORIA OF HESSE

SELECTED WITH A COMMENTARY BY

## Richard Hough

WITH A FOREWORD BY
THE PRINCESS'S GRAND-DAUGHTER

## The Lady Brabourne

SIMON AND SCHUSTER • NEW YORK

*Selection and commentary copyright © 1975 by Richard Hough*
*All rights reserved*
*including the right of reproduction*
*in whole or in part in any form*
*Published by Simon and Schuster*
*A Gulf + Western Company*
*Rockefeller Center, 630 Fifth Avenue*
*New York, New York 10020*
*Manufactured in the United States of America*
*1  2  3  4  5  6  7  8  9  10*


*Library of Congress Cataloging in Publication Data*

*Victoria, Queen of Great Britain, 1819–1901.*
  *Advice to my grand-daughter.*

  *First published in 1975 under title: Advice to a grand-daughter.*
  *Includes index.*
  *1. Victoria, Queen of Great Britain, 1819–1901. 2. Milford Haven, Victoria Alberta Elizabeth Mathilde Marie, Marchioness of, 1863–1950. I. Milford Haven, Victoria Alberta Elizabeth Mathilde Marie, Marchioness of, 1863–1950. II. Title. DA552.A38  1976    941.081'092'4*
*75-46597*
*ISBN 0-671-22242-2*

# List of Illustrations

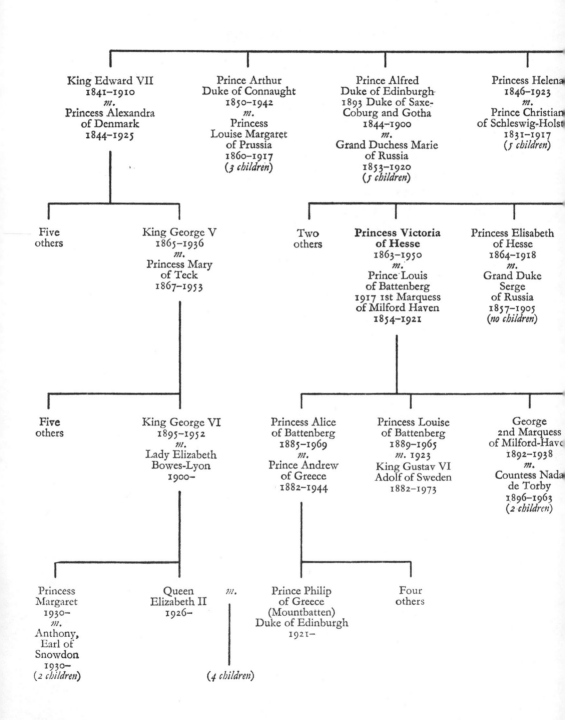

Queen Victoria
Empress of India
1819–1901

King Edward VII
1841–1910
*m.*
Princess Alexandra
of Denmark
1844–1925

Prince Arthur
Duke of Connaught
1850–1942
*m.*
Princess
Louise Margaret
of Prussia
1860–1917
(*3 children*)

Prince Alfred
Duke of Edinburgh
1893 Duke of Saxe-
Coburg and Gotha
1844–1900
*m.*
Grand Duchess Marie
of Russia
1853–1920
(*5 children*)

Princess Helena
1846–1923
*m.*
Prince Christian
of Schleswig-Holstein
1831–1917
(*5 children*)

Five
others

King George V
1865–1936
*m.*
Princess Mary
of Teck
1867–1953

Two
others

**Princess Victoria
of Hesse**
1863–1950
*m.*
Prince Louis
of Battenberg
1917 1st Marquess
of Milford Haven
1854–1921

Princess Elisabeth
of Hesse
1864–1918
*m.*
Grand Duke
Serge
of Russia
1857–1905
(*no children*)

Five
others

King George VI
1895–1952
*m.*
Lady Elizabeth
Bowes-Lyon
1900–

Princess Alice
of Battenberg
1885–1969
*m.*
Prince Andrew
of Greece
1882–1944

Princess Louise
of Battenberg
1889–1965
*m.* 1923
King Gustav VI
Adolf of Sweden
1882–1973

George
2nd Marquess
of Milford-Haven
1892–1938
*m.*
Countess Nada
de Torby
1896–1963
(*2 children*)

Princess
Margaret
1930–
*m.*
Anthony,
Earl of
Snowdon
1930–
(*2 children*)

Queen
Elizabeth II
1926–

*m.*

Prince Philip
of Greece
(Mountbatten)
Duke of Edinburgh
1921–

(*4 children*)

Four
others

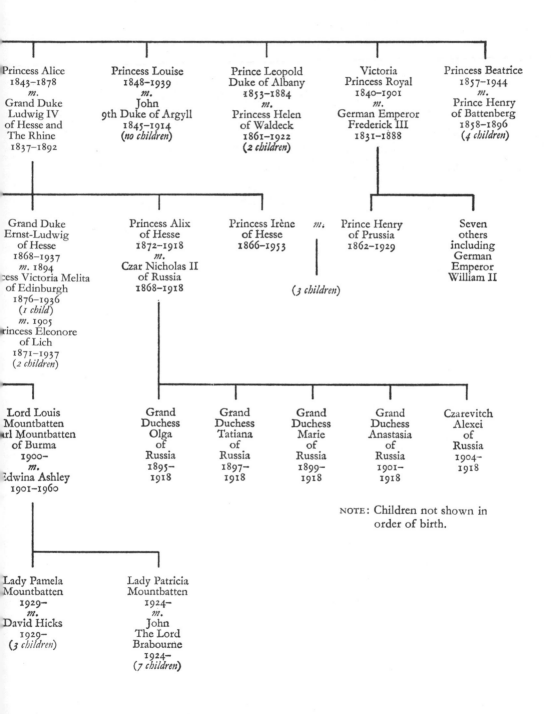

Prince Albert
of Saxe-Coburg
and Gotha
1819–1861

Princess Alice
1843–1878
m.
Grand Duke
Ludwig IV
of Hesse and
The Rhine
1837–1892

Princess Louise
1848–1939
m.
John
9th Duke of Argyll
1845–1914
(no children)

Prince Leopold
Duke of Albany
1853–1884
m.
Princess Helen
of Waldeck
1861–1922
(2 children)

Victoria
Princess Royal
1840–1901
m.
German Emperor
Frederick III
1831–1888

Princess Beatrice
1857–1944
m.
Prince Henry
of Battenberg
1858–1896
(4 children)

Grand Duke
Ernst-Ludwig
of Hesse
1868–1937
m. 1894
Princess Victoria Melita
of Edinburgh
1876–1936
(1 child)
m. 1905
Princess Eleonore
of Lich
1871–1937
(2 children)

Princess Alix
of Hesse
1872–1918
m.
Czar Nicholas II
of Russia
1868–1918

Princess Irène   m.
of Hesse
1866–1953

Prince Henry
of Prussia
1862–1929

(3 children)

Seven
others
including
German
Emperor
William II

Lord Louis
Mountbatten
Earl Mountbatten
of Burma
1900–
m.
Edwina Ashley
1901–1960

Grand
Duchess
Olga
of
Russia
1895–
1918

Grand
Duchess
Tatiana
of
Russia
1897–
1918

Grand
Duchess
Marie
of
Russia
1899–
1918

Grand
Duchess
Anastasia
of
Russia
1901–
1918

Czarevitch
Alexei
of
Russia
1904–
1918

NOTE: Children not shown in
order of birth.

Lady Pamela
Mountbatten
1929–
m.
David Hicks
1929–
(3 children)

Lady Patricia
Mountbatten
1924–
m.
John
The Lord
Brabourne
1924–
(7 children)

# Acknowledgements

I wish to acknowledge the gracious permission of the Queen to reproduce the Crown Copyright letters in this book, and for authorizing me to quote certain material from the Royal Archives at Windsor Castle. Her Majesty was also kind enough to allow me to include an observation she made to me about several people, including Queen Victoria's two surviving daughters whom she had known in her childhood.

The letters themselves are in the possession of the Broadlands Archives Trust at Broadlands, the home of Admiral of the Fleet the Earl Mountbatten of Burma. I am grateful to Lord Mountbatten and the Trustees for releasing them, and to Lord Mountbatten's daughter, and Princess Victoria's own grand-daughter, Lady Brabourne, for contributing a Foreword to this volume.

The Broadlands Archives also released for publication the illustrations in this book, and my debt to the Trustees is therefore a double one.

I also owe a great debt to Mr Robert Mackworth-Young, and Miss Jane Langton, Librarian and Registrar in the Royal Library at Windsor Castle, and to the late Commander Robin Bousfield, for their creative contributions to the manuscript as well as their conscientious checking of facts, dates, titles and so much else.

Finally, I thank Mrs Mollie Travis, Archivist at Broadlands, for all her patience and kindness.

February 1975                                    Richard Hough

# Foreword

## by The Lady Brabourne

My grandmother, to whom these letters were written, was the most remarkable person I have ever known. She illuminated my whole childhood and youth with a shaft of bright light which has kept her personality as strong an influence upon me now as it was at her death a quarter of a century ago. To spend any length of time with her, whether for an hour or a visit of several weeks, was always a joy, either as a child or as a grown-up. She had plenty of that rare and valuable commodity in today's rushed world – time – with which she liberally endowed her visitors. She knew how to amuse a child by making a fragrant soft ball out of cowslips, or a doll's teaset from acorns; how to put a nervous or retiring person at ease by finding out their interests; how to talk to an eminent professor or a high-ranking Service Officer on his particular subjects, about which she could often be better informed than they were. She dearly loved interesting conversation and was not averse to resounding arguments in several languages which never grew acrimonious, although they sometimes alarmed uninitiated listeners. Her knowledge was legendary; never, when she was in the house, did anyone have need of dictionary, atlas or encyclopaedia. You merely said 'Ask Grandmama', whose immediate answers were always full and fascinating. Her memory was prodigious and instantly brought history alive. What she had not lived through, she had read about voraciously.

And yet to a child she was in no way alarming because she had the gift of treating a child as an interesting person to be equally respected. I never remember wanting to be badly behaved with Grandmama, she was far too interesting and such behaviour would have been unthinkable and a waste of time. I greatly loved and admired her in every way: her courage, her philosophical and practical nature, her tremendous self-reliance, her intelligence and high standards. She was a very strong believer in the importance of family ties and support of each other, and yet she was totally independent and unpossessive herself.

There were times when my grandmother assumed more the role of a parent than grandparent to my sister and me. Coming as we did from a naval family there were long periods during the war and when my parents were stationed abroad, when they could not always have us with them. At such times our beloved grandmother would come to stay with us or we would visit her and the void would be temporarily filled.

Reading these letters I can appreciate how much good and sensible advice and help she received from her grandmother from childhood, although she was quite strong-minded enough not to heed the advice if she felt it was wrong. I well remember understanding what a special relationship these two remarkable women enjoyed, spanning two generations, from hearing my grandmother talk about hers. She certainly, although perhaps unconsciously, took over the same role with her own grandchildren and exerted a very strong and happy influence over our lives and personalities. This is probably why I have always believed very strongly in the importance of a good grandparent/grandchild relationship in a child's upbringing. I can only hope that when I find myself in the happy role of a grandmother myself I shall be able to some small degree to continue this tradition of a special relationship with my own grandchildren.

Patricia Brabourne

# Chief Characters

'AFFIE' see Alfred, Prince of Gt Britain and Ireland

ALBERT VICTOR, Prince of Gt Britain and Ireland ('Eddy' or 'Eddie') (1864–92) Duke of Clarence 1890

ALBERT, Prince of Gt Britain and Ireland ('Bertie') (1895–1952) Duke of York 1920. King George VI 1936

ALEXANDER, Prince of Battenberg ('Sandro') (1857–93). Prince of Bulgaria 1879. Count Hartenau 1889. Married Johanna Loisinger 1889

ALEXANDER, Prince of Battenberg ('Drino') (1886–1960). Marquess of Carisbrooke. Married Lady Irene Denison 1917

ALEXANDER, Prince of Hesse (1823–88) Father of Louis, Prince of Battenberg

ALEXANDRA, Princess of Denmark (1844–1925) ('Alix' or 'Alex'). Married Albert Edward, Prince of Wales 1863

ALFRED, Prince of Gt Britain and Ireland (1844–1900) ('Affie') Duke of Edinburgh 1866. Married Marie Alexandrovna, Grand Duchess of Russia 1874. Duke of Saxe-Coburg-Gotha 1893

ALICE, Princess of Albany, Countess of Athlone (1883–   ), Married Prince Alexander of Teck ('Alge') 1904, who in 1917 took surname Cambridge and was created Earl of Athlone

ALICE, Princess of Battenberg (1885–1969) Daughter of Louis and Victoria. Married Andrew, Prince of Greece and Denmark 1903

ALICE, Princess of Gt Britain and Ireland (1843–78) Mother of Victoria. Married Ludwig, Prince of Hesse 1862 who became Grand Duke of Hesse 1877

'ALICKY' see Alix, Princess of Hesse

'ALIX' or 'ALEX' see Alexandra, Princess of Denmark

ALIX, Princess of Hesse (1872–1918) ('Alicky'). Sister to Victoria. Married Nicholas II Emperor of Russia 1894

'ANDREA' see Andrew, Prince of Greece and Denmark

ANDREW, Prince of Greece and Denmark ('Andrea') (1882–1944). Married Princess Alice of Battenberg 1903

ARTHUR, Prince of Gt Britain and Ireland (1850–1942).

Created Duke of Connaught 1874. Married Princess Louise
Margaret of Prussia 1879

BEATRICE, Princess of Gt Britain and Ireland (1857–1944).
Married Prince Henry of Battenberg 1885

'BERTIE' see (Albert) Edward, Prince of Wales

'BOBBY' see Sigismund, Prince of Prussia

CHRISTIAN, Prince of Schleswig-Holstein-Sonderburg-Augustenburg (1831–1917). Married Princess Helena 1866

'DAVID' see Edward, Prince of Wales 1911

'DICKIE' see Louis, Prince of Battenberg

'DRINO' see Alexander Prince of Battenberg

'DUCKY' see Victoria Melita, Princess of Edinburgh and Saxe-
Coburg-Gotha

'EDDIE' or 'EDDY' see Albert Victor, Prince of Gt Britain
and Ireland

(ALBERT) EDWARD, Prince of Wales ('Bertie') (1841–1910)
Uncle of Victoria. Married Alexandra, Princess of Denmark
1863. King Edward VII 1901

EDWARD, Prince of Gt Britain and Ireland ('David') (1894–
1972). Prince of Wales 1911. King Edward VIII 1936. Abdicated 1936. Created Duke of Windsor 1937. Married Wallis
Warfield Simpson 1937

ELEONORE, Princess of Solms-Hohensolms-Lich (1871–1937)
('Onor'). Married Ernst-Ludwig, Grand Duke of Hesse 1905

ELIZABETH, Princess of Hesse (1864–1918) ('Ella') Sister of
Victoria. Married Sergius, Grand Duke of Russia 1884

'ELLA' see Elizabeth, Princess of Hesse

'ENA' see Victoria Eugénie, Princess of Battenberg

'ERNIE' see Ernst-Ludwig, Prince of Hesse

ERNST-LUDWIG, Prince of Hesse ('Ernie') (1868–1937)
Younger brother of Victoria. Grand Duke of Hesse 1892.
Married (1) Victoria Melita, daughter of Alfred, Duke of Saxe-
Coburg-Gotha 1894. Divorced 1901. Married (2) Eleonore,
Princess of Solms-Hohensolms-Lich

FRANCIS JOSEPH, Prince of Battenberg ('Franzjos') (1861–
1924) Younger brother of Louis. Married Anna, Princess of
Montenegro 1897

'FRANZJOS' see Francis Joseph, Prince of Battenberg

FREDERICK, Prince of Hesse (1870–73) ('Frittie') Brother of
Victoria

FREDERICK, Crown Prince of Prussia ('Fritz') (1831–88). Married Victoria, Princess Royal of Gt Britain and Ireland 1858. German Emperor 1888.

'FRITTIE' see Frederick, Prince of Hesse

'FRITZ' see Frederick, Crown Prince of Prussia

GEORGE, Prince of Battenberg ('Georgie') (1892–1938) Son of Louis and Victoria. Married Nada, Countess de Torby, daughter of Grand Duke Michael of Russia 1916. 2nd Marquess of Milford Haven 1921

GEORGE, Prince of Gt Britain and Ireland ('Georgie') (1865–1936) Cousin of Victoria. Duke of York 1892. Married Princess Mary of Teck 1893. Prince of Wales 1901. King George V 1910

'GEORGIE' see (1) George, Prince of Battenberg; (2) George, Prince of Gt Britain and Ireland

GUSTAV ADOLF, Prince of Sweden (1882–1973). Married Margaret, Princess of Connaught 1905. Crown Prince of Sweden 1907. Married (2) Lady Louise Mountbatten 1923. King Gustav VI Adolf 1950

HELEN, Princess of Waldeck and Pyrmont (1861–1922). Married Leopold, Prince of Gt Britain and Ireland 1882

HELENA, Princess of Gt Britain and Ireland ('Lenchen') (1846–1923). Married Prince Christian of Schleswig-Holstein-Sonderburg-Augustenburg 1866

HENRY, Prince of Battenberg ('Liko') (1858–96) Younger brother of Louis. Married Beatrice, Princess of Gt Britain and Ireland 1885

HENRY, Prince of Prussia (1862–1929). Married Princess Irène of Hesse 1888

IRÈNE, Princess of Hesse (1866–1953) Sister of Victoria. Married Henry, Prince of Prussia 1888

JULIE, Countess of Hauke (1825–95) Mother of Louis. Married Prince Alexander of Hesse 1851. Countess of Battenberg 1851. Princess of Battenberg 1858

'LENCHEN' see Helena, Princess of Gt Britain and Ireland

'LEO' see Leopold, Prince of Battenberg

LEOPOLD, Prince of Battenberg ('Leo') (1889–1922), Son of Prince Henry of Battenberg and Princess Beatrice. Lord Leopold Mountbatten 1917

LEOPOLD, Prince of Gt Britain and Ireland (1853–84) Duke of Albany 1881. Married Helen, Princess of Waldeck 1882

'LIKO' see Henry, Prince of Battenberg

LORNE, John Marquess of (1845–1914). Married Princess Louise of Gt Britain and Ireland 1871. Duke of Argyll 1900

LOUIS, Prince of Battenberg (1854–1921). Married Princess Victoria 1884

LOUIS, Prince of Battenberg ('Dickie') (1900–    ) Son of Louis and Victoria. Lord Louis Mountbatten 1917. Married Hon. Edwina Ashley 1922. Earl Mountbatten of Burma 1947. Viceroy and Governor-General of India 1947, 1st Sea Lord 1955, Chief of Defence Staff 1959–65

LOUISE, Princess of Battenberg (1889–1965) Daughter of Louis and Victoria. Lady Louise Mountbatten 1917. Married Gustav Adolf Crown Prince of Sweden 1923. Queen of Sweden 1950

LOUISE, Princess of Gt Britain and Ireland (1848–1939). Married John, Marquess of Lorne 1871

LOUISE MARGARET, Princess of Prussia ('Louischen') (1860–1917). Married Arthur, Prince of Gt Britain and Ireland 1879

'LOUISCHEN' see Louise Margaret, Princess of Prussia

LUDWIG, Prince of Hesse (1837–92) Father of Victoria. Married Alice, Princess of Gt Britain and Ireland 1862. Grand Duke Ludwig IV of Hesse 1877

MARIE, Princess of Battenberg (1852–1923) Elder sister of Louis. Married Gustav, Count of Erbach-Schönberg 1871

MARIE, Princess of Hesse ('May') (1874–78) Sister of Victoria

MARIE, Princess of Hesse (1824–80) Tsarevna of Russia 1841 on marriage to Tsarevitch Alexander. Empress of Russia 1855

MARIE Alexandrovna, Grand Duchess of Russia (1853–1920). Married Alfred, Prince of Gt Britain and Ireland, Duke of Edinburgh 1874

MARY, Princess of Teck ('May') (1867–1953). Married Prince George of Gt Britain and Ireland 1893. Princess of Wales 1901. Queen Mary 1910

MAURICE, Prince of Battenberg (1891–1914)

'MAY' see Marie, Princess of Hesse and Princess May of Teck

'MORETTA' see Victoria, Princess of Prussia

NICHOLAS, Tsarevitch of Russia ('Nicky') (1868–1918) Emperor of Russia 1894. Married Princess Alix of Hesse 1894

'NICKY' see Nicholas, Tsarevitch of Russia

OLGA, Grand-Duchess of Russia (1895–1918). Eldest daughter of Nicholas and Alexandra

'ONOR' see Eleonore, Princess of Solms-Hohensolms-Lich

PHILIP, Prince of Greece and Denmark (1921–    ) Grandson of Louis and Victoria. Duke of Edinburgh 1947. Married Princess Elizabeth, Heir Presumptive to the British throne 1947

'SANDRO' see Prince Alexander of Battenberg

SERGIUS ('Serge'), Grand Duke of Russia (1857–1905). Married Princess Elizabeth of Hesse 1884

SIGISMUND, Prince of Prussia ('Bobby') (1896–    ). Married Princess Charlotte-Agnes of Saxe-Altenburg 1919

'TODDY' see Waldemar, Prince of Prussia

'VICKY' see Victoria, Princess Royal of Gt Britain and Ireland

'VICKY' see Victoria, Princess of Prussia

VICTORIA Eugénie, Princess of Battenberg (1887–1969) ('Ena') Married Alfonso XIII King of Spain 1906

VICTORIA, Princess Royal of Gt Britain and Ireland ('Vicky') (1840–1901). Married Frederick, Crown Prince of Prussia 1858. Empress Frederick 1888

VICTORIA, Princess of Prussia ('Vicky', 'Cousin Vicky' or 'Moretta') (1866–1929). Married Prince Adolphus of Schaumburg-Lippe ('Adolf') 1890. Married (2) Alexander Subkov 1927

VICTORIA MELITA, Princess of Edinburgh and Saxe-Coburg-Gotha ('Ducky') (1876–1936). Married (1) Ernst-Ludwig, Grand Duke of Hesse 1894. Divorced 1901. Married (2) Kyril Vladimirovitch, Grand Duke of Russia

WALDEMAR, Prince of Prussia ('Toddy') (1889–1945). Married Princess Calixta-Agnes of Lippe 1919

WILHELM, Crown Prince of Prussia ('Willie' or 'Willy') (1859–1941). Married Princess Augusta Victoria of Schleswig-Holstein 1881. German Emperor 1888. Abdicated 1918. Married (2) Princess Hermine of Reuss

'WILLY' see Wilhelm, Crown Prince of Prussia

# Introduction

The letters in this book are from a most remarkable and complex woman, who was also Queen Empress ruling the greatest Empire the world has ever known, to a young and intelligent Princess from one of the oldest dynasties in Europe, Princess Victoria of Hesse and the Rhine, who died just twenty-five years ago.

The Hessians, stemming from the very heart of Europe and notable earlier in history for their military prowess, have enriched by marriage many of the Royal houses over many generations. In the nineteenth century their marriages into the Russian, Danish, Greek, Swedish, Prussian, Spanish and British Royal families, were particularly numerous, often beneficial and sometimes historically important.

Take the recipient of these letters alone. One of Princess Victoria's daughters married the future King of Sweden, another a Greek Prince who fathered Prince Philip, Duke of Edinburgh. Princess Victoria's elder son died tragically young but contrived to pack much into a short life, served gallantly in as many naval engagements as it was possible to serve in the First World War,[1] and has been described by Queen Elizabeth II as 'one of the most intelligent and brilliant of people'.

This Princess's younger son, now Admiral of the Fleet the Earl Mountbatten of Burma, has had a wider influence than anyone of his generation on monarchical and defence affairs in Britain, and has often been described as the most notable sailor since Nelson.

But, as so often with the Hessians, triumph could be bought only at the price of tragedy. Of Princess Victoria's four sisters, one died as an infant, one married a Prussian Admiral, which led to great difficulties when Britain and Germany went to war in 1914, and gave birth to two haemophilic sons. Another sister married a reactionary Russian Grand Duke who was assassinated

---

[1] It has been calculated that, in the course of the Battles of Heligoland Bight, Dogger Bank and Jutland, Prince George's twelve-inch gun turret fired more rounds than any other turret on either side.

twelve years before the Russian Revolution, when she herself was horribly murdered.

The Princess's last sister married the Emperor of All the Russias. The whole world knows how she was murdered by communists, along with her husband, her four daughters and her haemophilic son, the Tsarevitch.

Queen Victoria died before many of these Hessian tragedies had occurred – before the divorce of the Princess's brother, the Grand Duke himself; the death of his beautiful daughter at the age of eight; the divisive consequences of world war; and the virtual destruction of the ancient Hessian family in an air crash in 1937.

But Queen Victoria, who on the one hand was so preoccupied with tragedies of her past, with dreadful coincidences and dreaded anniversaries, preserved throughout her long life a sharply pro- phetic eye and highly developed intuition. This led her to per- ceive the dangers that lay ahead, so that she did all within her power to prevent marriages with families which might soon be- come involved in revolution or in hostile acts aimed towards the British people.

Before the Queen died in 1901, a revered but disconsolate figure, after the longest reign in British history, she knew she had failed in many of her marriage plans. 'I feel very deeply that my opinion & my advice are never listened to,' she wrote to her grand-daughter in one moment of despair, '& that it is almost useless to give any.'

But she could console herself that she had fought the good fight to the end, just as she knew Princess Victoria had done what she could to direct her younger sisters into less hazardous mar- riages.

In the complex web of nineteenth-century European dynasties, Princess Victoria's genealogy is comparatively simple. In 1862 Queen Victoria's second daughter Alice had married Prince Lud- wig of Hesse, heir to the Grand Dukedom. The wedding took place in the dark shadows cast by the death of Princess Alice's father, Prince Albert, Consort to Queen Victoria. Alice had been very close to her father, in some ways closer than the Queen her- self. She had inherited his solid virtues, nervous intensity and total lack of humour; and had nursed him with tender care through his fatal illness.

Queen Victoria remembered lovingly and gratefully her daughter's attention to Albert when he was dying; yet she was also jealous of the special understanding between her husband and her daughter. She resented Alice's rallying efforts when she continued for so long and so vocally her expressions of bereavement, just as she resented Alice's comparatively brisk attitude to personal tragedy when it came to herself – and it did come in abundance after she married her Hessian prince.

Princess Victoria (1863–1950) was born while her grand-mother was still stunned by the loss of Prince Albert. This may have been one reason for the special measure of affection the Queen felt for this grand-daughter, which grew ever stronger until the Queen died thirty-eight years later.

Princess Alice's early ordeals, first as Princess of Hesse and then as Grand Duchess, included the Grand Duchy's war with Prussia and a now-united Germany's war with France in 1870–1. While she cared for the wounded and dying on both sides, in-spired by the example of her friend Florence Nightingale, she agonized over the fate of her husband, who was in the forefront of the fighting, like any good Hessian.

Domestic troubles followed in rapid succession. Like at least two – and perhaps three – of her sisters, Princess Alice was a 'carrier' of haemophilia, that dread royal bleeding disease which Queen Victoria (to her horror) had passed on to her children of both sexes. One of Princess Alice's sons died during a fall as a result of haemophilia, and two of her own daughters (as I have shown) proved in later life to be 'carriers', too.

When Princess Alice succumbed at thirty-five, worn out in mind and body, in an especially virulent diphtheria epidemic, which looked at one time as if it might wipe out most of the family (and did kill her youngest daughter), Princess Victoria took on the formidable duties of foster mother to her three younger sisters and younger brother. No fifteen year old could have been better fitted for the responsibilities. The letters she received from the Queen at this time not only offer sound advice but reflect the poignancy and bitterness of the Hessian ordeal as it affected her.

But while Princess Victoria read, and took in her grand-mother's recommendations and guidance like the sensible girl she was, this matter-of-fact, tomboyish, practical little golden-haired

Hessian got on with the business of guiding her sisters and brother in the family and regal duties that lay before them, supported always from afar by the magisterial and matriarchal figure of Queen Victoria herself.

'Look on me as a mother,' the Queen repeated time and again to her grand-daughter as she chivvied and cajoled, guided and disapproved and encouraged the young girl until she became a young woman.

Some people may think that advice contained in letters to a Hessian Princess more than a century ago is scarcely relevant to the problems of growing up into a much-changed world today. But in fact only a little of it is of a trivial and ephemeral nature. The rest relates to any girl from her seventh birthday (when these letters begin) to any woman of thirty-eight, when these letters fade out in Queen Victoria's last hazy months of extreme old age.

There are, besides, in these letters numerous comments and sidelights on domestic, national and international events, which fill in, however slightly, the elaborate portrait of this immensely interesting Queen which continues to be added to even today.

Princess Victoria missed her grandmother dreadfully when she died in 1901. The rest of the Princess's life was devoted to bringing up her own children, attending to her relations in Germany, Russia and England, and supporting her husband, who rose to the top in the Royal Navy and partnered Winston Churchill at the Admiralty on the outbreak of war in 1914.

She shared his suffering when he was hounded out of office by 'the death-or-glory Beresford boys and the cushy-job journalists of the Yellow Press',[1] and when he was even forced in the xenophobic tidal wave to change his rank and name in 1917.

Princess Victoria, now as the Dowager Marchioness of Milford Haven, outlived Prince Louis by almost thirty years. She was never for one moment idle, even in old age. Among her responsibilities, shared with others of her family, was the care of her grandson Prince Philip until he joined the Royal Navy in 1939.

The greatest satisfactions of her old age, which Queen Victoria

[1] Sir Iain Moncreiffe of that Ilk reviewing *Louis and Victoria: the First Mountbattens* by Richard Hough in *The Spectator*, 30 November 1974.

would have enthusiastically shared, were, first to see her surviving son become a war hero and Supreme Commander of the South-East Asia campaign and emerge successfully from the India Vice-royalty; and, four years later, to see her grandson marry the future Queen of England.

Only a handful of the earliest letters from Queen Victoria to the young Princess Victoria of Hesse have survived. It is likely, in any case, that the Queen wrote to her only for her birthdays, a practice she followed with all her grandchildren, children, relatives and close friends; although for the little ones there might also be short notes at Christmas or the New Year.

A modest gift would accompany these birthday letters, which often contained a special personal note, for the Queen was almost incapable of writing a banal or stereotyped letter to anyone on any occasion.

Princess Victoria's birthday was 5 April, 1863. The first two of these letters, then, are in response to the Princess's 'thank you' letters. Until she was ten years old the Hessian family remained free from the tragedies that beset them periodically from 1873 until the air crash at Ostend in 1937.

OSBORNE

April 28 1870

Darling little Victoria,

Your dear little letter gave Grandmama great pleasure & she sends you a kiss for it.

It is very nicely written. Grandmama hopes dear Mama will some day let you stay for some time with her in England.

I see by your photographs how much you and Ella[1] are grown.

I wish you could see the thousands of beautiful primroses – we have here! The grass and banks are covered with them & the nightingales sing beautifully.

I send you now a photograph of Aunt Beatrice.[2]

Ever your devoted old Grandmama
Victoria R.I.

[1] Princess Elizabeth (1864–1918), her next younger sister.
[2] Princess Beatrice, Queen Victoria's last child (1857–1944).

April 18 1871

Darling little Victoria,

Your beautifully written letter has given Grandmama the greatest pleasure and she thanks dear little Victoria very much for it. I am so glad to hear that you like the pearls & the paint box.

I am very sorry dear Papa has left you again and you must miss him sadly.

I shall send a print to Katrinchen which Mama said she would like to have. You are very sorry to lose her I am sure.

It will be a great pleasure to Grandmama, Auntie Beatrice & Uncle Leopold[1] if you can come to see us this autumn.

Give sisters and brothers a kiss from Grandmama

Ever your most affectionate Grandmama

Victoria R.I.


BUCKINGHAM PALACE
April 2 1873

Darling Victoria,

On this your *10th* Birthday Grandmama writes to wish you many many happy returns.

May you grow daily in goodness & strive more & more to be a comfort to dear Papa & Mama. You will miss them both very much & they will miss you.

My presents are 2 pearls & a workbox which I hope you will like. Give my kindest love to dear Ella, Irène & Ernie & a kiss to Fritzie & Baby.[2]

Pray also give my kindest love to your dear Grandmama, Grandpapa[3] has I think left you.

Ever your devoted Grandmama

V.R.I.


Queen Victoria's letter for Princess Victoria's eleventh birthday makes reference to the first of the Hessian tragedies which

[1] Prince Leopold (1853–84), the Queen's last son. He was a haemophiliac but married in 1882 Princess of Waldeck and Pyrmont. Their elder child, Princess Alice, Countess of Athlone, lives today in Kensington Palace.

[2] Princess Victoria's other younger sisters and brothers, Princess Irène (1866–1935), Prince Ernst-Ludwig (1868–1938), Prince Frederick (1870–3), Princess Alix (1872–1918) and Princess Marie (1874–8).

[3] Prince Charles of Hesse (d. 1877) and his wife, formerly Elizabeth of Prussia (d. 1885).

scarred the Princess's life almost until her death after the Second World War. Her mother was a haemophilia 'carrier'; and, like Uncle Leopold, Fritzie (or Frittie), the youngest Hessian boy, was a haemophiliac. In the course of a boisterous game with his elder brother, Fritzie fell from a window. It was not a great fall, and a normal child might well have survived it. He died of an effusion of blood on the brain. Like many haemophiliacs, the boy was especially lively and happy, and the tragedy nearly broke his mother's heart. It also instilled in Princess Victoria a fear of the disease which lasted all through her life.

OSBORNE

April 5 1874

Dearest Victoria,

Let me wish you many many happy returns of this day which I hope you have spent happily with dear Papa & Mama & your brother & sisters! But one dear little face will be missing who was with you last year! *He* surely gives you his blessing from above where he is happy & free from pain & sorrow!

I hope you liked the pearls & *watch*? It belonged to me as a child – & as it has a V on it – I thought it would do for you.

Ask dear Mama to have that engraved inside, as well as that it had been given me by my dear Aunt Louise of Belgium.

I hope that you are growing in goodness in every way & are a very obedient good child & a comfort to Papa & Mama.

Give my affectionate love to Grandpapa & Grandmama & a kiss to Ernie & the sisters.

Ever your very affectionate Grandmama

V.R.I.

While the Queen accepted her dynastic responsibilities in full and encouraged her children and grandchildren to make happy and advantageous marriages abroad, she felt every absence deeply, welcomed them warmly for long visits, could take offence if they came too seldom and stayed for too short a time, and always deeply regretted their departure. With every good reason, she regarded herself as the greatest matriarchal figure among Europe's royal dynasties. With less accuracy, she also saw herself as a shrewd and benevolent spider weaving the complex genea-logical webs that should strengthen the Royal families and bring happiness to her relations and consolidate the power of the 'good' nations to the detriment of the 'bad' nations – like Russia.

The Queen best of all liked to have her young relations at beloved Balmoral where there were few distractions and her guests were unlikely to be lured away by her elder sons the Prince of Wales ('Bertie') or Prince Alfred ('Affie'), whose influence, she suspected, was not always as morally uplifting as it should be.

The collie Noble to which the Queen refers was one of a veritable tribe of dogs, all loved and none disciplined, which assumed a prominent part in the Queen's domestic life, and provided her with a perennial subject of interest in her letters to young relations.

BALMORAL CASTLE

June 11 1875

Darling Victoria,

Your dear letter received yesterday afternoon gave me great pleasure. We miss you very much & think of you wherever we go! I hope we shall have you again here some day to cheer us & make us merry.

You know that when good Brown[1] bid you goodbye he said 'Haste ye back' which is the Highland expression for 'Come back soon again' – We had a good deal of rain in the afternoon of the day you left, a beautiful day on Tuesday, a good deal of rain on Wednesday, & a beautiful day yesterday and we took a long drive – 7 miles beyond the Linn of Dee where we thought of you – & only came home at ¼ past 9! But it was quite light still and very fine. Tomorrow is a week already since the gay Ball!

I am so glad you found Brother & Sisters well. Give them & dear Ella a kiss from me. Noble is quite well again & now goodbye & God bless you. Don't forget old Grandmama[2]

Ever your devoted Grandmama

V.R.I.

BALMORAL

Oct 5 1875

Darling Victoria,

Many thanks for your nice kind letter recd. since I came here. Being here makes me think much of you both & the happy time you spent

---

[1] The Queen's Scots gillie, who gave her such support after the death of Prince Albert in 1861.

[2] She had just passed her 56th birthday.

here with us – We came back last week from a visit to Inverary of a week – where dear Aunt Louise & Uncle Lorne[1] are living wh. is a very fine place. I have brought you each a little box from there with views of it.

Aunt Helena[2] left yesterday mng as well as Uncle Leopold. Dear Uncle Arthur[3] is still here but leaves on the 8th & the week after for Gibraltar & I shall not see him for a long time. Uncle Bertie also leaves on the 11th for his long & distant journey to India.[4]

I must end to go out, sending many kisses to Irène, Ernie, Alicky & May.

Ever your loving Grandmama<br>V.R.I.

Tell dear Mama I can't write today but send some views of Inverary

BALMORAL

June 5 1876

Dearest Victoria & Ella,

Your dear letters & the mat you & Irène worked gave me great pleasure & I only wish that you could have been here with me as last year to enjoy this fine place & to be at the Ball which is given tomorrow.

But my birthday & arrival here were saddened by the death of your dear Aunt Lenchen's little boy.[5]

Uncle Leopold was much pleased to see dear Mama and Ernie & will now have been with you all at Darmstadt.

We have not had very fine weather. Much wind – a cold wind – & very changeable weather. It was very hot on the 1st & 2nd & then poured & turned colder.

[1] The Queen's fourth daughter Louise married John, Marquess of Lorne, in 1871. He succeeded as 9th Duke of Argyll in 1900 and died in 1914. The Duchess lived until 1939. It was not a happy marriage. (See footnote page 21.)

[2] Princess Helena ('Lenchen') (1846–1923) was the Queen's third daughter, and in 1866 had married Prince Christian of Schleswig-Holstein.

[3] Prince Arthur (1850–1942) was the Queen's third son and, with the exception of Prince Leopold, the most intellectually well endowed. He married Princess Louise of Prussia in 1879.

[4] This refers to the Prince of Wales's state visit to India. Victoria's future husband, Prince Louis of Battenberg, accompanied the Prince as an orderly officer and contributed many drawings of the tour to *The Illustrated London News*.

[5] Prince Harold of Schleswig-Holstein, born 12 May, died nine days later.

I have been driving & walking & taking our tea out. We are expecting Cousin Leopold, King of the Belgians, here on Wednesday for 2
days.

On the 20th or 21st we go back to Windsor. Thank dear Papa very
much for his kind letter & say I had no time to write. Give Irène, Alicky
& dear little May many kisses. Tomorrow is dear Alicky's birthday. All
your photographs are charming & so like.

I am so glad to hear you like the pony

Ever your devoted Grandmama

V.R.I.


Almost the last surviving letter (*below*) before further catastrophe
overwhelmed the Hessian family was written when Victoria was
about to be fourteen. If the Queen had known what was in store
for them all in 1878 she would not have referred to 1877 as a sad
year. The 'loss' incidentally refers to the death of Prince Charles
of Hesse.

The Queen now regards Victoria as a young woman who more
than ever requires firm guidance. There is little doubt that she
feels a special measure of love and regard for her, correctly
discerning exceptional qualities of mind as well as weaknesses,
like a tendency to be dogmatic and argumentative, which will
have to be corrected.


OSBORNE

April 3 1877

Darling Victoria,

These lines are to wish you every possible happiness for your dear
birthday which last year we had the pleasure of celebrating with you at
Darmstadt! Alas! this year will be a sad one after the loss of your dear
excellent Grandpapa. Your poor dear Grandmama will have so sad &
lonely a life & I am sure you & your sisters will do all you can to
comfort & cheer her!

My presents to you are 2 pearls & a locket for your dear Grandpapa's
hair.

May God bless you & may you each year grow in goodness & more
& more be a comfort & happiness to your Parents & all belonging to
you.

Try to be humbleminded, unselfish, truthful & loving to all, with a
firm trust in our Heavenly Father & His Guidance.

You will be delighted to have Ella with you again & to see good Miss Graves back again. Again wishing you joy & God bless you

Ever your devoted Grandmama

V.R.I.

Love to Sisters & Brother.


On the evening of 8 November 1878 Victoria was reading aloud to her younger sisters and brother. Her throat was sore but she dutifully carried on, only complaining of it later to 'Orchie', Mrs Mary Anne Orchard, the family nurse. The doctor was called in and diagnosed diphtheria. The dread disease, in a very virulent form, rapidly spread to the rest of the family, except Ella, and the mother, Princess Alice (now the Grand Duchess of Hesse). Victoria recovered quite rapidly, but the other children were very ill and little May ('Sunshine' to the family) died on 16 November. The Queen despatched Sir William Jenner to Darmstadt.

At one time the Grand Duchess, herself a resolute and experienced nurse, was helped by eight more nurses and doctors, who treated the family and the Grand Duke with inhalers and chlorate of potash.

One by one the others recovered, and prayers of grief for the lost Princess, and of thanks for the recovery of the rest of the family, were said all over Hesse.

At one time the mother, already physically and spiritually weary, and further exhausted by worry and grief, had kissed her surviving son on the forehead. It was the British Prime Minister, Benjamin Disraeli, who called this the 'kiss of death'. A few days later, the Grand Duchess contracted the disease. She knew she would never recover.

During the second week in December, telegrams that became more and more frantic flashed between Windsor Castle and Darmstadt. On the morning of 14 December, the anniversary of the death of Prince Albert and the day she dreaded more than any other, Brown brought the Queen a last telegram announcing the death of her second daughter.

'That this dear, talented, distinguished, tender-hearted, noble-minded, sweet child, who behaved so admirably during her dear father's illness,' wrote the Queen in her Journal, 'and afterwards, in supporting me in every possible way, should be called back to

Windsor Castle.

Dec: 14. 1878.

Darling Victoria,

Poor dear Children
for I write this for
you all, — You
have all had these
most terrible blow
Dhila camberfale
Children — You have
lost your precious
dear, devoted Mother

her father on this very anniversary of his death, seems almost incredible and most mysterious.'

Later in the day the Queen wrote this letter to Victoria, doubly underlining 'the terrible day' in the date.

WINDSOR CASTLE

Dec 14 1878

Darling Victoria,

Poor dear children, for I write this for you *all* – You have all had the most terrible blow which can befall Children – you have lost your precious, dear, devoted Mother who loved you – and devoted her life to you & your dear Papa! That horrible disease which carried off sweet little May & from which you & the others recovered has taken her away from you & poor old Grandmama, who with your other kind Grandmama will try & be a Mother to you! Oh! dear children, dearest beloved Mama is gone to join dear Grandpapa & your other dear Grandpapa & Fritte & sweet little May where there is no more sorrow or tears or separation.

I *long* to hear every detail! Poor dear Ernie, he will feel it so *dreadfully*! May he & dear Papa not suffer from this dreadful blow.

Try & do everything to comfort & help poor dear Papa! God's will be done! May he support and help you all.

From your devoted & most unhappy Grandmama

V.R.I.

Let Ella see this letter.

OSBORNE

Dec 27 1878

Darling Victoria,

Thank you very much for your last dear letter – Time seems to make our dreadful loss only greater & you will feel day after day more and more the irreparable dreadful loss your darling Mama is to you! You are fast growing up & wd. have become so much of a companion to her – who was so devoted to you all, loved you so – was so anxious for your good – & gave her precious life for you all!

You must treasure her in your hearts as a *Saint* – one who is rare in this World! It is a great *privilege* to be her child, but it is also a gt. responsibility to become *really worthy* of her – to walk in her footsteps – to be unselfish, truthful, humble-minded – *simple* – & to try & do *all* you can for *others* as *she* did! Ask dear Papa to show you the newspaper articles I sent him, wh. are *all* beautiful! – Think always (as you do) how blessed & happy precious Mama is *now* with Frittie & darling May & her *own* dear father!

This must have been a dreadful Christmas & *what* a New Year! That every blessing may be yours in this new & terribly altered year is the earnest prayer of your loving, devoted & sorrowing Grandmama

VRI

There are many reasons for the Victorians' deep preoccupation with death, and the unrestrained and ostentatious style in which they greeted it in speech, in writing and no doubt in their true feelings, too. No one was a more ardent exponent of this 'permissiveness' of the mid-Victorians than the Queen herself, although at a time when death was much nearer to everybody, she was comparatively unscathed in her immediate family, apart from the loss of her husband while she was still only forty-two. None of her children died in infancy at a time when this was commonplace and only three of them died in her own long lifetime. (Three lived into their eighties and nineties.)

Princess Alice, Grand Duchess of Hesse, for whom the Queen now mourned, had herself been comparatively stoic in bereavement and had come as near as anyone to rebuking her mother for her prolonged anguish over the death of Prince Albert.

As the Hessian family began to adjust itself to its new loss, the Queen, while bent on cherishing and consoling her grandchildren, was equally determined that they should mourn for their lost sister and mother '*more* and *more*', if not for a lifetime then for many years to come.

Early in the New Year the entire family was invited to Osborne and Windsor Castle for a bereavement sojourn. After their return to Germany on 28 February the Queen in her letter of 3 March refers to Prince Leopold's latest accident – always a grave worry with a haemophiliac – and to Prince Arthur's marriage to Princess Louise of Prussia.

But after this happy event, the Queen is cast down into grief again. From Italy she writes (2 April 1879) of a further family death from diphtheria, this time of the fourth son, Prince Waldemar of Prussia, of her eldest daughter the Princess Royal ('Vicky').

OSBORNE
Jan 14 1879

Darling Victoria,

Two letters I have received from you but never the one thanking me for mine.

It is today a month since that most dreadful day which shattered your happy home. It seems *impossible* it can be so long. In a week, please God! you will be with us! *What* a meeting! I trust you will be comfortable. After severe cold we have since yesterday a thaw & today deluges of rain.

Let me thank you very much for your work & dear Irène too. It is so pretty.

Poor dear Ernie I am so glad he is better. How sad he must feel! I *will write* to Papa tomorrow & if possible to Ella too. I am to see Fr Helmsdörfen[1] tomorrow.

Love to dear Papa & Brother & Sisters. Have you been to the Rosenhöhe[2] lately?

Ever your devoted sorrowing Grandmama<br>V.R.I.

WINDSOR CASTLE
March 3 1879

Darling Victoria,

It seems already so long since you left us – & we miss you so much! What a dreadful return it must have been & how you must miss darling Mama! I had not an opportunity before you went to say how I hope you will try more & more to be a help & comfort to dear Papa, & try to make his dreary life less desolate & to do *all* you can to improve in every way. You have still much to learn of course & I hope you will always be very ready to follow what Miss Jackson[3] & also Wilhelmine[4] tell you – for you have no longer the blessing and advantage of a loving watchful Mother. At your age kind advice is of the greatest importance for the future & I am sure your greatest wish will be to follow in your darling Mama's footsteps & do what she wd have liked.

How very unfortunate your Uncle Leopold having hurt his leg! I was so afraid of this happening & it wd be most unfortunate if he was unable to be back for Uncle Arthur's wedding!

---

[1] The head of The Alice Hospital, which Princess Alice had established in Darmstadt. She nursed the princess during her fatal illness.

[2] The family mausoleum of the Hessians in Darmstadt.

[3] 'Madgie' governess to the Hessian girls.

[4] Wilhelmine von Grancy, a lady-in-waiting who helped with the children.

Remember me kindly to Wilhelmine & Miss Jackson & kiss dear Sisters & darling Ernie. Auntie Beatrice sends you many loves. We have fine spring weather with a hot sun but frosts at night. How is the little dog & the cat & her family?

Ever your loving Grandmama<br>V.R.I.

Give my kind love to Grandmama. We miss you all *terribly*.

VILLA CLARA, BAVENO

April 2 1879

Darling Victoria,

Let me begin by wishing you many many happy returns of your dear birthday, your *16th* which will I fear be a most sad day for you all – without your precious Mama, who would have been so happy on this day. Three years ago we spent it so happily with you at Darmstadt on such a beautiful day – & *how* well do I remember your birth at Windsor when dear Mama spoke of dear Grandpapa with whom she is now again. Sweet little May too, how you will miss her! My presents are two pearls, a bust of dear Mama & a book all of which I hope you will like!

But oh! This *dreadful new* misfortune breaking out in your dear Aunt Vicky's family – and taking away her dear, clever, promising boy Waldie!! *Too, too awful!* Auntie Beatrice sent Bäurelein [Bäuerlein] a letter yesterday from Ctss. Brühl[1] which I wish her to show to Papa & Uncle & you all. And I enclose a letter from Mme. de Perpigna[2] written *before* that wh is also for all of you to see and which please return to me. I have the most heartbroken & touching letters from poor dear Auntie Vicky. It is such agony to have lost that dear Boy & to feel still anxious for a few days about the others! How this has damped this interesting journey you may well believe.

Many many thanks for all your dear letters which always give me such pleasure. Uncle Leopold will I am sure have told you all about my journey which I wrote at full length to him.

This is a beautiful enchanting spot. This mng. and during the night it has rained a good deal & it is still raining but it is clearing & we are going to visit the Isola Bella. The views are quite magnificent such glorious mountains all around & the quantities of camellia bushes, in fact trees covered with flowers is quite astounding. There are myriads

[1] Countess Brühl was Lady-in-Waiting to the dead boy's mother, the Princess Royal.

[2] Governess to the Princess Royal's daughters.

of primroses too and quantities of beautiful Evergreens but the common trees are not more forward than in England.

Do scold good Herr Müther[1] for not writing once to me. He was to write *once* a fortnight. He will be so saddened at darling Waldie's death. And Wilhelmina & Miss Jackson have only written once each! Tell Ernie I am so glad little Charlie gets on so nicely. I am only sorry the poor cat is dead but hope the kittens will thrive.

When are you going back to your dear Home? You *must* press dear Papa very strongly to go back this month. Thank Sisters for their dear letters.

Again praying that God may bless protect – keep & guide you ever in the right path & make you as good, loving straightforward & God fearing Child or rather more *Girl*, for you are fast growing out of a Child.

Believe me always your devoted Grandmama

V.R.I.

This is a most comfortable charming house.

WINDSOR CASTLE

May 14 1879

Darling Victoria,

As I have not written to you for some time I write to *you* instead of to dear Papa today & ask you to thank him for *his* letter & to give him this extract as well as this copy of Ld Salisbury's[2] letter to me.

Many thanks for your 2 dear letters of the 26th & the 27th. How sad & desolate everything *must* be! I miss writing to & hearing from darling Mama dreadfully!

And what must it be to you missing her daily, hourly. Poor dear Papa *how* I feel for him!

I went on Wednesday last in London to see the Monument & it is beautiful. Little May is so like now. It is almost too touching to look at!

We were so very very sorry to leave Baveno & the beautiful Lago Maggiore & the enchanting country all round & I am quite glad to think we shall soon see mountains again.

You will be surprised & pleased to hear of Cousin Charlotte's Baby!

We saw Miss Byng[3] on Monday & she is still weak. Uncle Leopold has had a very bad sore throat but he is well again.

I send you today the lithograph wh I had done of dear Mama & wh I am sure you will like. There is one for dear Papa & for each of you.

[1] Tutor to Victoria's brother, Prince Ernst-Ludwig.

[2] 3rd Marquis of Salisbury (1830–1903), notable Conservative statesman.

[3] The late Prince Waldemar's governess who was recovering from diphtheria.

On Wednesday next 21st we are going to leave for Balmoral. Uncle Leopold & 2 of the little girls of Uncle Bertie are going with us.

We expect the Empress of Germany in abt an hour & so I must end

Ever your loving old Grandmama

V.R.I.

T.O. Pray thank Herr Müther for his kind letter wh amused me very much. I just find that the lithographs cannot be sent till tomorrow.

BALMORAL

May 29 1879

Darling Victoria,

Your dear letter for my poor old birthday touched me very much & I thank you so much for it as well as for the Head which is really beautifully done! Oh! *how* sad was that mng!! How I missed darling Mama, her letter, her gift – her telegram. From *all my* other children I heard but *not from her*! It quite overwhelmed me & when I got dear Papa's & your letters how my heart sank within me! It was too terrible. How I *do* miss her & *you* poor dear children must feel it more & more! To try & be like her – unselfish & courageous, loving & good – that is how best to fulfil her dear wishes & to keep living on with her. Desolate & sad as the dear House is – I am so glad to think you *have* returned there. You must feel much nearer to her there. The sad sad picture dear Papa gave me of the Rosenhöhe makes me understand how it all is now, & I value it much.

Cousins Louise & Maude[1] of Wales are here with us & Uncle Leopold is here too They will leave us (that is Cousins) I believe next week.

Poor dear Papa I am sure you try all you can to be a help & comfort to him!

How is he? Did you do that Head from a cast or from a drawing?

Our weather is still very unsettled tho not really cold. Everything is coming out very slowly especially the Birches & all the higher hills have large patches of snow & the highest are almost quite white at the top.

We expect your cousin Sandro Battenberg[2] now Prince of Bulgaria here next week. His birthday is the same as yours.

It is very wrong of the English to be all going away from Darmstadt. Uncle & Auntie send you their best love & believe me

Ever your devoted Grandmama

V.R.I.

[1] First and third daughters of the Prince and Princess of Wales.
[2] Prince Alexander of Battenberg, Victoria's future brother-in-law.

Cousin Charlotte's[1] baby is to be called Feodore after Bernard's step mother Feo who was sister to Uncle Hermann Hohenlohe.

What a *sad sad* day this is again.[2] How well I remember the agony of it for poor Darling Mama.

WINDSOR CASTLE

July 4 1879

Darling Victoria,

I recd your dear letter this mng & as I wrote to dear Papa yesterday I send you this enclosure to show him & ask you to send it me back as soon as possible. You & Ella may also read it. It is *too* sad! The troop ship Orontes bearing the dear remains has reached Madeira today & may be expected D.V. on the 10th quite early at Spithead.[3]

I am so glad you like Wolfsgarten[4] But *how* much you must miss *darling* Mama every where! I do so dreadfully, her dear letters so full of thought & affection! You must *try* & *write* what you feel & think too as you get older. Tell dear Papa also that the Bust by Kopp of dear Mama is come & quite beautiful so much improved by the alteration.

We have awful weather such storms of wind & such deluges of rain. No one can go on the grass

Ever your devoted Mama[5]<br>V.R.I.

OSBORNE

Aug 6 1879

Darling Victoria,

I have again alas! been long without writing – but there has been so much to do & to write – so many painful anxious subjects to take up my time that I have neglected what I wished most to do.

Many loving thanks for your dear letters of the 18 July & 1st. How everything here reminds me here of beloved Mama. The long lower

---

[1] The Princess Royal's eldest daughter and wife of Prince Bernhard of Saxe-Meiningen.

[2] The anniversary of the untimely death of Victoria's younger brother.

[3] A reference to the death of the Prince Imperial of France, only son of ex-Empress Eugénie, in the Zulu War, 1 June. See also letters of 6 August and 14 October.

[4] The Hessian summer palace north of Darmstadt.

[5] In view of the Queen's frequent request to her Hessian grandchildren to regard her as a mother, this may have been a conscious mistake.

alcove where I am now sitting is where we took tea the day she arrived here last year the 16th (I think) & oh! *how* I long for her – miss the constant intercourse with her! The dear family picture is a great delight & comfort to me & so wonderfully – splendidly painted & grouped – so very like. I think Ella's expression is *just* hers & Ernie's an expression he very often has.

The funeral at Chislehurst was terribly sad but not gloomy the coffin being covered with the 2 flags & many flowers – the Artillery men seated on it holding a wreath the many uniforms – all prevented its being gloomy tho' that dreadfully sad 'Dead March in Saul' with the minute guns went thro & thro one. The poor dear Empress's grief is one almost too sacred to approach. But she bears it with such beautiful resignation & is so kind & forgiving to every one – blames no one! I send you some of the Illustrations from the Graphic in case you have not seen them which you can keep amongst you.

Today is Uncle Alfred's birthday, he with Aunt Marie & the dear little children are living at Osborne Cottage where Uncle Arthur & Aunt Louischen[1] are staying just now for a few days. And Uncle Bertie & Aunt Alix with the 5 cousins are on board the 'Osborne'[2] at Cowes. The Ponsonby's[3] are at Kent House[4] where dear Sir Thomas & Ly [Lady] Biddulph were last year. Uncle Leopold is nearly well again. He went to Boyton[5] on Thursday & will come here on the 15th.

I am glad Willie[6] paid you a visit. I send Papa by today's messenger a book which I think will interest him on the Cape by Miss Hardinge's brother in law. Miss Protheroe is quite well & greatly flattered at your enquiries. The old people at the Alms House are also quite well.

I wrote to dear Papa the other day about your confirmation & I have no doubt he will speak to you about it. Will you tell him that Mr Teignmouth Shore[7] was here last Sunday & is now going to Hambourg & Darmstadt.

---

[1] The Queen's seventh child, Prince Arthur, Duke of Connaught had married in 1879 Princess Louise ('Louischen') of Prussia. (See also footnote 1 on page 37.)

[2] One of the Royal Yachts.

[3] General Sir Henry Ponsonby, Private Secretary to the Queen 1870 to 1895.

[4] Kent House, later bequeathed to Victoria who lived there with her husband in the First World War.

[5] A rented house in Wiltshire.

[6] The future Kaiser Wilhelm II.

[7] The Rev. Teignmouth Shore, whose sermons Princess Alice had greatly admired. He was appointed Hon. Secretary of the English Princess Alice Memorial Fund.

And now with many loves to Sisters & Ernie & kind remembrance to Wilhelmina & Miss Jackson & some kind words to all the others.

Ever your devoted Grandmama

V.R.I.

I hope Ernie will be very obedient. I am vy. glad Ella's foot is well again.

Queen Victoria, always a great one for anniversaries, writes to her grand-daughter with ever-growing anguish as summer turns to autumn and the first anniversary of the death of Victoria's mother approaches. The merciful healing processes of the Hessian children after their bereavement have little chance against these recurrent reminders from England of the grief the Queen feels sure they must be suffering. It says much for the girls' resilience that they quite rapidly recovered from their loss and returned to their normal cheerful style.

The child who suffered worst was almost certainly Ernie, who had endured terrible nightmares after the death of his young brother five years earlier. The news of the death of his little sister May was kept from him for as long as possible. He was thrown into paroxysms of grief when he was at length told. For a boy as sensitive and highly-strung as he was, the further blow of the death of his mother was terrible indeed.

Ernie and his father were again invited to Britain in the summer so that the Queen could console them in their loss. They stayed at Balmoral where the Grand Duke forgot his worries stalking deer on the moors, accompanied by his son who was nearly eleven years old. Ernie was more an intellectual than an extrovert sportsman and no doubt derived less consolation from stalking than his father did.

Victoria herself is again reminded of the new responsibilities thrust upon her by the death of her mother. The references to world events are a sign that the Queen recognizes that she is no longer a child and will soon be a woman, with dynastic responsibilities before her. Here is the first evidence, too, of the Queen's determination to prevent any of her Hessian grandchildren from marrying into hated Russia – a prospect so feared and so important that it grows almost into an obsession.

BALMORAL CASTLE

Sep 12 1879

Darling Victoria,

I wrote in such a hurry I cd not thank you for your dear last letters of the 22nd & 23rd of Aug. of the 4th & 9th of Sept. Today is dear Papa's birthday of which I wish you many & happy returns but for him it will be dreadful! I am sorry he cannot be with you but for *him* being quite away is no doubt better.

Darling little Alicky's drawing is quite delightful in its originality & dear Ernie's little letter amused me very much. Thank him for it & Irène for hers.

How I often wish to see you dear children. How long it seems since we parted & till we can meet again. But Miss Jackson gives me very good accounts of you. You will however miss a Mother's care love & devotion more & more as life goes on! Did you see Mr Shore & speak at all to him? He is a very kind man. I was glad you saw Gnl. Hardinge, Lord Sydney & the [indecipherable].

As yet we have no reason to think the Ameer had anything to do with the awful massacre.[1]

We have heard most interesting accounts of the war in Zululand from Lord Chelmsford who was here for 3 days last week & from Sir C. Wood & Col Buller[2] & other most distinguished Officers who came here on the 9th & left this mng.

I will write to Ella in a day or 2. Christel & Abby[3] are at [illegible] with their schoolmaster.

Ever your devoted Grandmama<br>V.R.I.

BALMORAL CASTLE

Sept 23 1879

Darling Victoria,

I send you today 4 new photos for you, Ella, Irene & Alicky which I hope you will like. Get 4 frames for them & let them go abt with you. Many loving thanks for your dear letter of the 17th. It brought the tears to my eyes! For it is so sad – terrible to think of you darling children

---

[1] A reference to the troubles in Afghanistan. British residents in Kabul had been massacred on 3 and 4 September.

[2] The Zulus were finally subjugated this year. Buller (1839–1908), later Field-Marshal and C.-in-C. in the Boer War, won a V.C. in this campaign.

[3] Princess Helena's boys, Prince Christian Victor of Schleswig-Holstein, and Prince Albert.

being without precious beloved Mama! How I long for her & *how impossible* it seems to me that *she* shd be gone from this world. Poor dear Papa it is indeed sad he shd be so often away! I wish I cd be with you often, and then unfortunately your lessons prevent your being as much with him as he & I wd wish.

I *hope* you will not get at all Russian from the visits to Jugenheim![1] Dear Mama tho loving the language had *such* a horror of Russia & Russians! I am sorry Mr Shore cd only stay so short a time. I must end for today.

Ever your devoted Grandmama<br>V.R.I.

BALMORAL CASTLE

Oct 14 1879

Darling Victoria,

Many loving thanks for your 3 dear letters which gave me much pleasure. I am so glad to see that Russian ways are not to your taste but very sorry that Grand Aunt Marie of Russia is[2] so weak & poorly.

You may well imagine the mingled pleasure & pain it is to me to have dear Papa here without beloved Mama & that the sight of dear Ernie, her only boy, to whom she so clung & so doted on (tho. not less on you *all*) looking so strong & well, unberufen,[3] is a gt. pang at times.

Dear Papa is also looking so well. He has been very lucky stalking & has killed (I think) 14 stags. We have been on 3 long & very pleasant expeditions together.

Poor Aunt Marie E.[4] has had a little boy who died at once, wh will be a great disappointment. The accts. of her are very good however. You must be rather dull in town & not able to get much out & sad & lonely in thinking of this time last year when dear Mama was still with you.

It is terrible to think of the coming sad days! To see her rooms just the same & she not there must be too terrible!

The Queen Empress has been very often it does her real good to be here. But poor thing she is brokenhearted.

We shall be very very sorry to see Dear Papa & Ernie go but I rejoice for you.

[1] The Russian royal family, with its numerous connections with the Hessians, often stayed in the summer at Heiligenberg Castle, Jugenheim, the seat of the Battenbergs south of Darmstadt.

[2] The Empress of Russia, Prince Alexander of Hesse's sister. She died the following year.

[3] Touch wood.

[4] Daughter of the Russian Empress, who married Queen Victoria's son, Prince Alfred.

Love to all & to dear Grandmama to whom I will try to write by dear
Papa

Ever your devoted Grandmama

V.R.I.

Nov 4 1879

Darling Victoria,

I have not written as soon as I intended but I had no time. I can't tell
you the pain it was for me to part from dearest Papa whom I love so
much & pity so truly! And darling Ernie too! And just at this moment
when every day will be an anniversary, the dear House will be full of the
saddest recollections! On the 6th you became ill, on the 8th darling
Mama telegraphed in the greatest anxiety that you were ill with Dyph-
theria then on the 11th that you were out of all danger only to be
*followed* by the fearful and ever succeeding days & weeks of anxiety
anguish sorrow & mourning when precious Mama bore up with such
such heroic resignation & courage.

After 2 bad days we have again the most heavenly weather! We are
going to the Glassalt Shiel again today for 3 or perhaps 4 nights. The
poor Empress was very sad to leave Abergeldie & feels very wretched
again at Chislehurst.

With love to all & thanking you for your last dear letter in wh. you
*don't* thank me for mine.

Ever your devoted & loving Grandmama

V.R.I.

I send Papa a photograph

Dec 12 1879

Darling Victoria,

I write these lines to arrive on that *dreadful* day wh took your darling
Mama as well as 17 years before your darling Grandpapa away from
their happy homes. Unfortunately you had not, as dear Mama had had,
the blessing & privilege of being with her during her illness & at the
*last*, when she passed away, as she had of being with her beloved Parent
to the last moment & of seeing him while ill. And I was near my *own*
beloved Mother when she died. *This* I grieve for your sake was denied
to you – as you were not able to have that blessed & sacred recollection
of it for life! But as life goes on and you get older, & require the support
& advice of a loving Mother you will more & more feel the terrible

loss! Let *every* day bring you nearer to her & to her dear memory. Think how she gave her life out of love for you all!

Be all you can to poor dear Papa & your brother & sisters. So much depends on you darling Victoria as the eldest.

We shall all go to the Mausoleum for a short service there at 11.30 on the morning of the sad 14th and in the aft'noon at evg. Service in the Chapel here. Mr T. Shore will preach.

God bless you darling child, you know you can always look on me as on a Mother

Ever your devoted Grandmama
V.R.I.

T.O. How every day *now* reminds me of this terrible time last year – living between hope & fear! Speak to the others *from me*!

WINDSOR CASTLE
Feb 27 1880

Darling Victoria,

I have to thank you for several dear letters of the 2nd & 14th of Jan & 4th & 13th. It will be a *great* satisfaction to me to be able to be present at your & Ella's confirmation & I trust that nothing will occur to prevent it. It will be a terrible trial for me to go to Darmstadt & *not* to find beloved Mama. It makes me very nervous. To be with you & dear Papa I feel quite a duty. But the visit to the Rosenhöhe will [be] *vy vy* sad & trying.

I am so glad that dear Papa has consented to your being confirmed in white as dear Mama & your Aunts were.

Poor dear Aunt Louise had a dreadful accident[1] & is I fear still very far from recovered, tho going on well. The shock was terrible and how dreadful was that event at St Petersburg.[2] Too awful! It must have shocked dear Papa, Grandmama & Pss. Battenberg[3] dreadfully. Uncle Alfred is gone there to see Aunt Marie & also for the Emperor's 25th Jubilee.

[1] The capsizing of a sleigh in which she and Lord Lorne were riding. She was dragged by her hair for some distance and lost an ear. She never recovered her happy relationship with her husband, who at that time was Governor-General of Canada.

[2] An assassination attempt on the Emperor of Russia. Prince Alexander of Hesse and his sons Alexander and Louis (Victoria's future husband) were in the party whose train was delayed and thus all escaped by a hairsbreadth the mighty explosion of a bomb.

[3] Victoria's future mother-in-law.

A very sad thing happened here yesterday. Dr Fairbank who attended the Household here & Aunt Helena & was a very gt friend of hers died suddenly of apoplexy! He was driving up to see her at Cumberland Lodge when he was taken ill & became unconscious: they drove him up to C. Lodge (*not* to Aunt's *House*) & then he rallied for a time when he became suddenly worse & died there. His poor wife & Aunt Helena were present. She is very much upset & distressed & he is a *gt loss* to her.

Herr Sell's sermon I liked particularly. I am sure he has prepared both of you well.

Poor Gnl. Scudamore's death is very sad. It must have been a gt & painful trial for poor dear Papa to go to the Opera & I pity him for it.

We have dear Uncle Alfred's darling little children here wh is a gt pleasure. They are such lovely children.

Pray thank dear Papa for his last letter & tell him about poor Dr Fairbank. I hope Ernie has not eat [*sic*] too many 'sweeties' again! Give all my tenderest love. Ever your devoted Grandmama

V.R.I.

How sad it is that Marie Erbach's 2nd child is so delicate.

Through the Queen's advice and exhortations the reader acquires an ever clearer view of the young Princess. It is evident that she was at this time far from being 'posée', which means steady, sober and quiet. She also talked far too much and far too loudly. In spite of the Queen's efforts, Victoria remained un-posée and garrulous all her life. It has often been said that all the Queen's daughters[1] were tremendous talkers, and certainly the present Queen recalls that her great-great aunts, Princess Beatrice and Princess Louise, were great talkers even in their old age. This garrulity was inherited by many of the grand-daughters, more especially Princess Victoria of Hesse herself, perhaps the greatest Royal talker of them all. Her son Earl Mountbatten of Burma claims that only three people ever succeeded in stopping his mother talking: Queen Victoria, her husband Prince Louis of Battenberg who was known sometimes to burst out, 'My dear child, will you kindly SHUT UP!', and himself – 'I sometimes won by persistence.'

[1] See the letter from Queen Victoria of 15 July 1890 (page 107).

VILLA HOHENLOHE, BADEN BADEN

Ap 4 1880

Darling Victoria,

May *every every blessing* be showered on you on your dear 17th birthday
& may you have *strength* given you to be that support & help to your
dear Papa wh he so *gtly needs*! *Every, every* where you see what your
beloved Mama did – how she worked for your country, watched over
& led everything & how she stood by & supported your dear Papa –
& you must try to follow in her footsteps – Modestly, unpresumingly,
*not* putting yourself forward too much but being *always* ready to help &
ready to do *at Home* what Papa wishes & requires.

You must learn to be *posée*, not talk too much or too loud – but take
your place as your beloved Father's eldest daughter deprived of your
beloved mother!

It is the *greatest misfortune* wh cd befall you & your dear Sisters – but
if you trust in God's help & keep fast to the *solemn* vows wh you took
at your Confirmation, if you are humble minded & loving to all &
occupy yourself with serious things, you will succeed. Be always *ready*
to *listen* to the *advice* of *those* whom you *know* to be *truly devoted* to you –
& *not* to those who will flatter you & wish to do what *you* may like, but
wh often may be *bad* for you. My prayers for your *good* will be unceasing.
Since I have *been in* your Home I see better than ever *what* you have *all*
lost!

I was *dreadfully* upset by it all but so thankful to have been there!

My presents are 2 pearls – a box from here & a print you liked.

With many loves to dear Papa & all

Ever your most devoted Grandmama

V.R.I.

I was so pleased to *lead you* to your confirmation. Thank Miss Jackson
for her letter.


WINDSOR CASTLE

July 5 1880

Darling Victoria,

Your dear letter was such a pleasure to me this mng. We do miss you
sadly for, for us, it is much worse than for you who have had the
happiness of finding your dear Papa & darling Sisters & Ernie, who
Miss Jackson says were *so* delighted to see you again!

I am thankful the dear doggies kept well & are approved. Everything
has gone on the same but on Friday & Saturday we had constant violen
& heavy showers so we had to take tea in the Cottage.

Since yesterday it is quite fine. I wish you cd both see the 3 lovel

Collie puppies wh arrived here today – Noble's gd children born at
B. Palace gardens – Such loves – very like what Collie & her brother
were when we saw them at Loch Callater last October. These are 7
weeks old just a day younger than Floe's [*sic*]¹ at the Shaw Farm but
much bigger – black & tan. Ella would be in extacies [*sic*] over them.
We have just been hearing Mr Leslie's splendid Choir 190 strong who
sang in St George's Hall.

Eddie & George² came on Saturday evg & stopped till this mng.
They burnt almost all my pastilles & *also* some grass!! 'to keep off the
midges' making little bonfires in different directions.³

The Empress Augusta seems rather distressed at not having seen you.
Perhaps some day Papa cd take you over to see her some day [*sic*] for she
is really devoted to dear Mama's memory & to you too. On a journey
these visits are really dreadful.

I must end for today but will write next to Ella – tomorrow if possible.
*How* I love you darling children, how *dear* you are to me & how I look
on you as *my own* I can hardly say – *You* are so doubly dear as the
children of my *own* darling Child I have lost & loved so much – tho you
were always so very dear to me! If only dear little May had been spared
to be a companion later to Alicky.

Kissing you both warmly

Ever your devoted Grandmama

V.R.I.

Brown said on Friday morning that it seemed all wrong without you &
as if 'a Blight had come over us'. Auntie is quite well again.

FROGMORE GARDEN

July 17 1880

Darling Victoria,

I write here under the Trees (in gt heat) where we spent so many
happy hours together to thank you for your dear letter of the 10th.
Since the 12th the heat has been very great such vy [word illegible]
steamy, thundery heat-thunder almost every day.

¹ Flo, a terrier dog. It is unlike the Queen to misspell the name of a dog!

² The Prince of Wales's two sons, Prince Albert Victor and Prince George.
At this time they were sixteen and fifteen years old.

³ The Windsor and Balmoral flies appear to have been especially virulent.
Princess Victoria, a lifelong smoker from this time (the future Kaiser first
tempted her), was once asked by the Queen to 'light up' to keep away the
midges although she thought the Queen did not know she smoked secretly in
the Royal palaces. (You certainly did not smoke *openly*!) The Queen even took
a puff out of curiosity and found it distasteful.

The Review was beautiful – Uncle Bertie looked so well in his Uniform on his Charger at the head of the 3 Household Cavalry Regts! 10,000 men were there – the 2 Divisions from Aldershot. But ½ an hour or an hour after it was over a dreadful thunderstorm came on with torrents of rain wh lasted off & on the whole night & on into the morning. Yesterday it thundered again but at a distance & without rain.

You were right to be shocked abt Bradlaugh[1] & you will be as much at the shameful Vote agst the dear Pce. Imperials' monument in the H. of Commons agt Mr Gladstone & Sir S. Northcote! It is disgraceful. Would you explain to dear Papa abt dear Mama's engraving? I merely wished to know if he had an autograph to lend me & send me *here* (as it must be done here on template) with her 3 names or if he thought 'Alice' alone with 1878 wd be best? *Aunts* have their 3 & 4 names but not Uncles.

Please ask him to telegraph. I hope Pet is becoming obedient. She must be well 'haundled'[2] as Brown says. The little ones at the Shaw Farm are delightful & so are the little Collies now at the Kennell [*sic*].

Poor Uncle Leopold was imprudent & overdid it fishing & had both legs bad! Why will he not listen?[3] Auntie sends many loves

Ever your devoted Grandmama

V.R.I.

Princess Victoria sometimes shocked her grandmother with her tomboyish ways. The Queen disapproved strongly of young women (and Victoria was now seventeen) 'riding rough horses', which she regarded as unfeminine and bad for their health and well-being. Also, to go out with the guns was one thing but '*only fast* ladies' actually shot.

Although there is a reference to Victoria seeing Prince Louis of Battenberg in the next letter, their ardent love affair had not yet developed. In fact, Prince Louis was having a passionate affair with Lillie Langtry at this time.

[1] Charles Bradlaugh was a radical Member of Parliament who refused to 'take the oath' and eventually won his right to take his seat and 'affirm' instead of swearing on the Bible.

[2] The Queen is evidently imitating Brown's Scotch accent.

[3] This unfortunate but charming haemophilic son of the Queen suffered many painful and dangerous haemorrhages in his last years and was a constant source of the Queen's anxiety. She attempted to shield him from danger by prohibiting him from almost every activity and agonized over his frequent accidents. Elizabeth Longford describes the Queen as being 'hopelessly over protective'.

OSBORNE

Aug 4 1880

Darling Victoria,

Many thanks for your 2 dear letters of the 21st & the 31st. I send you today a print of Pss Charlotte, also like you, & then you shall have the Photograph after the Picture in my room as soon as a good one is taken.

I am so delighted to hear that the Pictures promise to be so like, tho I am sorry for the time they take. I am very curious to see them. Tell dear Papa I will write to him tomorrow or next day & that I thank him very much for his 2 dear letters.

We saw Louis B. [Battenberg] on Sunday & you will I suppose see him in three days as he is going back directly. Uncle Bertie, At Alix & the girls are living on board the Osborne again. Uncle Arthur & Aunt Louischen are here since the 31st & stop till the 8th – Uncle Leopd. will be here D.V. on the 10th or 11th & At. Louise comes with him but goes on to Germany at once –

The news from India are most distressing and many most valuable lives are lost! –

I was, darling Child, *rather* shocked to hear of your shooting at a mark but far more so at your idea of going out shooting with dear Papa. To look on is harmless but it is not lady like to kill animals & go out shooting – & I *hope* you will never do that. It might do you gt harm if that was known as *only fast* ladies do such things.

I must end. Ever your devoted Grandmama

V.R.I.

Love to all.

BALMORAL

Oct 5 1880

Darling Victoria,

I recd your dear letter of the 2nd today & thank you very much for it, as well as for the previous one of the 9th Sept. We are so happy to have dear Papa – sisters & Ernie here – & count the days we can still keep them. We have had beautiful warm weather till Saturday when as well as on Sunday we had snow & hail showers. Yesterday was beautiful but cold & today is so too.

We have been on several charming long expeditions & yesterday evng. there was a Ball at Abergeldie to wh we all went. Perhaps I may have one *here* still before they all go, in the Ball-room –

I have often heard of Ranke's 'Popes'[1] but thought it was rather a heavy book.

[1] Leopold von Ranke's *History of the Popes* which Victoria had asked her grandmother to read.

There is a very interesting little acct. of the War in Zululand, that is, the history of the rise of it, & an acct of the dreadful battle of Isardhl-wara & Rorkes Drift wh. you wd. like. Pray send me a Photograph of Elizabeth of Hesse[1] don't forget yours with your dogs.

I must end rather in a hurry but not without saying that I *quite* share your opinion about the poor Turks. It is a terrible business owing to Fröhlichstein.[2]

Love to Ella

Ever your devoted Mama [*sic*]

V.R.I.

BALMORAL

Oct 26 188c

Darling Victoria,

I could not answer your dear letter of the 19th by messenger but thank you now much for it.

Today is the Christening & I hope little Victor[3] will have behaved well. I wd like to telegraph but don't know where to – 27th. I was prevented from finishing my letter yesterday which I do today. I was very pleased to get the Telegram from dear Papa & the Erbach's after the Christening & hope to get letters from you giving me an acct. of the whole.

We have very severe weather – ever since the day dear Papa left, wh is so unusual so early in the year. It prevents long walks or drives wh is most tiresome. On Monday the snow was mostly gone & these two last nights it has returned again – tho' not so much.

How pleased you must be to have sisters & brother back again. It must make the House so bright again. But soon will come the sad & terrible time of that dreadful *illness* wh brought such sorrow & such a misfortune over you all. How I miss Darling Mama! Her dear letters wh I have been looking over lately – fill me with such a longing for that correspondence which was *such* a pleasure. That austausch der Gefühle und Gedanken[4] was so delightful.

I hope *you*, as the oldest sister will *see* that the younger ones are very punctual abt their lessons – for I am sorry to say *all* 3 tried to evade

[1] Elizabeth, Princess of Hesse-Cassel, who was three years older than Victoria's sister Ella, with whom she should not be confused.

[2] One of the Queen's pejorative nicknames, Merry Pebble, for Mr Gladstone, whom she cordially detested.

[3] Count Victor Erbach-Schönberg, second son of Count Gustav and Prince Louis's sister Marie. He was born 26 September 1880.

[4] Exchange of sentiments and thoughts.

them when they were here, & poor Herr Müther, was, *with right*, very much annoyed at Ernie's laziness & constant wish to avoid his lessons wh was not the case last year – & he requires to work hard & steadily now for he is very backward.

Thank Miss Jackson for her letter & ask good Wilhelmina to write to me.

With many kisses to the dear Geschwistern[1]

Ever your devoted Grandmama

V.R.I.

T.O. We shall have the Halloween on Monday & on Tuesday go again to the Glassalt Shiel

Queen Victoria understood, better than any contemporary monarch, the dangers of extravagance and flamboyance at court. The mainspring of her life, reflected in the style of upbringing of her own children, was built on self-reliance, self-discipline and God-fearing austerity. The dissipation and corruption in the French court, to say nothing of Hanoverian extravagance even closer to home and closer in time, were awful examples to her of court life run to seed and dissipation. Her husband, 'Dear Albert', added further strength to her resolution which so strongly influenced the whole manner of life of middle-class Britain for several generations.

She detested and was fearful of the ostentatious and spend-thrift ways of the Russian Romanoffs, and regarded with distaste the over-stiff and over-protocol-conscious Prussians. Their inflexible monarchical ways, she shrewdly and percipiently believed, would be their own undoing. Now that the Queen had heroically, but gladly, taken on the responsibility of the motherless Hessians ('think of me as your Mother' she constantly beseeched Victoria), she was determined that they should all grow up as her own daughter Alice would have wished them to be brought up, *posée*, well-mannered, well-educated, wise and restrained in their ways.

These Hessian grandchildren must not rush into marriage too early 'for marrying's sake' or 'to have a position'. She did not want them to marry Prussians. Above all else, they must on no account marry Russians. The happiest outcome would be for them all to marry well, in England, preferably to their own

[1] Brothers and sisters.

cousins. That way they would strengthen family ties – a laudable thing in itself – and she could keep her eye on them, and their children.

WINDSOR CASTLE

Dec 8 1880

Darling Victoria,

I cannot tell you *what* pleasure your dear affte. letter of the 14th gave me! It shows so *much* good sense & *right*, proper feeling – as well as such confidence in your old loving Grandmama who loves you as a Mother & *wishes* to be *one* to *you as much* as she possibly can. God bless you for it sweet Child! Beloved Mama, excepting Auntie Beatrice (& she was & is too young to understand many things wh only a wife & Mother can) was *the one* of my daughters who *felt with me* so much, & agreed with me in her views about my Children & I think I can therefore tell you *what she* wd. have *wished* –

You are right to be civil & friendly to the young girls you may occasionally meet, & to see them sometimes – but *never* make *friendships*; girls friendships & intimacies are very bad & often lead to great mischief – Grandpapa & I never allowed it, & dear Mama was quite of the same opinion. Besides, as you so truly say, you are so many of yourselves that you *want no one* else. I think also that you are *quite* right *not* to have large parties for you are both, & Ella, decidedly too young for them. And at the dinners remember *not* to talk too much & especially *not* too loud & not *across the table*.

I am so glad to hear that you are getting on with Italian.

There is another *most important* thing wh you are *quite old* enough for me to speak or write to you about. Dear Papa will, I know, be teazed & pressed to make you marry, & I have told him you were far too young to think of it, & that your 1st duty was to stay with *him*, & to be as it were the Mistress of the House, as so many eldest daughters are to their Fathers, when God has taken their beloved Mother away – I know full well that *you* have *no* ideas of this sort & that *you* (unlike, I am sorry to say, so many *Princesses abroad*) – don't wish *to be married* for *marrying's sake* & to have a *position*. I know darling Child that you would *never* do this, & dear Mama had a horror of it; but it is a very *German* view of things & I wd. wish you to be *prepared* & on your *guard* when such things are brought before Papa, & possibly to your Grandmama.

Write to me as often & as openly as you like about *everything* & it will be my *greatest pleasure* as well as my greatest *comfort* to be of use to you. It will be something like writing to darling Mama, & it would give *her* such pleasure.

The state of Ireland causes me the greatest anxiety & worry! Uncle Leopd. is able to walk about on crutches now – & we expect him here next week.

Now goodbye & God bless you Darling Child. This day two years ago I first heard of darling Mama's illness & on Tuesday is that *terrible* anniversary.

Love to Sisters & Ernie & thanks to him & Ella for their nice letters.

Ever your most devoted Grandmama

V.R.I.

OSBORNE

Feb 7 1881

Darling Victoria,

I am afraid I have been dreadfully remiss in writing to you but have had so much to do – that I have got very irregular abt. my correspondence – Many thanks for your dear letters of the 15th 20th & 30th Jany. I am so thankful dear Grandmama is better but till her eyesight has recovered more entirely you must feel anxious. Dear Papa seems afraid to admit how ill she was. Mr Scott also telegraphs almost daily – May God spare her valuable life to you all! Poor dear Children without darling Mama – who have you besides dear Papa but your 2 Grandmamas?

I am thinking now so much of seeing you again & hope dear Papa will allow you to come & go with us to Scotland again & then stay on a little bit afterwards.

Your accts. of the gt. dinner interested me very much – I hope you have read the accts. in the Times of the dreadful scene in the H. of Commons with that Irish Member? Last week there were the most fearful scenes & Mr Gladstone has been well punished for his gt. violence in opposition. But he is *now* doing his very best to restore order & authority & the opposition have supported him admirably, so different to the other Party.

About Kandahar,[1] I am very anxious & still hope it may not be given up. We have trouble with the Boers of whose connection with the Irish Land League etc. there is no doubt.

We are also threatened with a new Ashantie [*sic*] War – so that our anxieties & troubles are *endless*!

Dear Papa will I hope [have?] told you what I wrote to him of the dreadful snow? We were cut off every where – & even now (& it has

[1] General Roberts had relieved this besieged town in Afghanistan the previous August. It was again threatened.

been thawing & quite warm with rain since the 27th) – there are places in the lanes – above a foot deep of hard snow!

Yesterday was very fine but it turned cold & today it is *snowing again* after 13 deg: of frost! However I think it is half sleet half snow – Aunt Helena paid us a little visit from Thursday to today – What *sort* of girl is Elizabeth of Hesse? She is not pretty is she? And is she not *very* lively & fond of all sorts of amusements?

How is Miss Jackson? She complains very much of her hand & was ill. Thank Wilhelmine very much for her kind letter.

Did she go with you to Carlsruhe? Is Victoria of Baden as nice as ever?

Love to sisters & Ernie

Ever your devoted Grandmama

V.R.I.


OSBORNE

Aug 3 1881

Dearest Victoria,

My warmest thanks for your 2 dear letters of 15th & 27th July & for the fly bottles or bowls wh. arrived on Monday – & wh. shall be tried. I send you today some photographs of the Review to divide between you, Ella & dear Papa –

I can send more if you wish & I will send next week some very nice ones of the bridge over the River – Since the 19th when the heat reached a climax of unbearableness it has become very unsettled – & often quite cool in the evng. & at *night* tho' only really pleasant. We have had lately a gt deal of wind & some days rain – Sunday it poured & then rained almost all day.

We are a very large (rather too large) family party here in the neighbourhood), for one can't enjoy one another – Uncle Affie & Aunt Marie & the sweet lovely children are at Osborne Cottage & the children come every mng. to see us – Uncle Bertie & Uncle Fritz[1] are gone to London till tomorrow on acct. of a gt. international medical meeting wh. takes place in London this week. The accts. of the dear Empress Queen are better but this is such a dreadful year that one trembles when one hears of any one being indisposed –

Dear Lady Fanny Baillie has been dreadfully ill during the last 10 days – but since yesterday the eruption has gone & the temperature is below normal. She must have caught it fm. the Dean – Poor Victoria

[1] The Prince of Wales's brother-in-law and future German Emperor Frederick III. He was married to the Queen's eldest daughter Vicky.

B. [-aillie ?]– it has been a terrible trial & anxiety for her. Have you begun reading Kingsley's life? How do things get on with Miss Jackson?[1]
I am always anxious to hear. Have you seen any of the articles on dear
Dean Stanley? They are very interesting. I send one from a Scotch paper
wh. I wish you to give Uncle Leopd. to whom I will write today or
tomorrow. I am overwhelmed & overdone with work.

   The acct. of dear Grandmama makes me anxious. If she has grown
thin & pale so suddenly, I think that not a good sign – Thank dear Papa
for his kind, sad letter wh. I will answer soon.

Ever your devoted Grandmama<br>V.R.I.

Aunt Louise is here since Monday.


BALMORAL CASTLE

Aug 27 1881

Darling Victoria,

   Many loving thanks for 2 dear letters. Arrived here this mng. at 8.45 –
we feel as if we must see you again dear Children! In the breakfast room
especially – it seemed as if you must be sitting there!

   Our weather in Edinburgh was simply dreadful. We had a gt. deal &
constantly recurring rain at Osborne & arrived on Wednesday mng. in
Edinburgh in perfect deluges – the crops lying flat & unripe – the burns
like torrents. And so it continued more or less all day. We visited the
new & splendid Royal Infirmary that afternoon. The town was gaily
decorated & tremendously full. On Thursday mng. everything was in
bustle & excitement – only gter from being a large town – as at Windsor
on the day of the Review[2] – Quite early the sun shone; then it clouded
over but remained fair – & all was hope for at least a fair or even only a
showery or misty afternoon. But instead of that just *before* we started
for the Review it came down in torrents & continued the whole time
like a long 2 hours thunder shower, too dreadful! *Every* one drenched
to the skin. Still it was a splendid sight – 40,000 men numbers in kilts &
such fine men & showing such endurance & perseverance! Terrible for
them to have to go back *all* wet! Uncles were drenched & Uncle
Arthur's ribbon of the Thistle *went* thro' his red coat on to his shirt!!
In spite of umbrellas & waterproofs we also came in for our share of

---

   [1] After their mother's death the Queen saw a change for the worse in her
character and conceived a growing dislike for her.

   [2] The Queen reviewed the Scottish Volunteers in Queen's Park, Edinburgh,
in a continuous downpour.

   (In two months time the Queen would have reigned longer than Queen
Elizabeth.)

wet, impartially. Aunt Marie[1] especially had her whole back *wet*, thro' her stays!!

In the evng. we had a large Dinner & yesterday mng. it was fair so we drove up to the old Castle – the position of wh. is so fine, where is shown the room in wh. James VI of Scotland & first of England was born.

I now wish to say a word seriously abt. dear Ernie. Herr Müther has given me an acct. of the studies & I must say Ernie's gt. absence, in-attention & backwardness are becoming serious in his position & at his age.[2] I have not yet written abt. it to Papa but I think he ought to go away for 2 or 3 months with Herr Müther where he cld. have no *distractions* & learn steadily without the hope of picnics & expeditions wh. occupy his mind far too much. You should speak to Herr Müther & then to dear Papa & we must all urge something being done.

It is the highest time. Many loves to all
Ever your devoted Grandmama<br>V.R.I.

BALMORAL CASTLE
Oct 28 1881

Darling Victoria,

I enclose a few lines for Ella for her birthday. Many affte. thanks for your nice long letter of the 16th with the very interesting & *not* sharp acct.[3] of the guests at Carlsruhe. You must be glad to have dear Papa again – for you must feel so lonely & lost without him.

Have you heard from Vicky[4] of Sweden since she got to Stockholm. They are now staying at a place of their own wh. seems to give them great pleasure.

What books are you reading now & what masters have you got? I hope you have looked into the books I gave you & begun Kingsley's life?

A people's Edition of dear GdPapa's life is being published now. The whole will only cost 2s 6d wh is wonderful.

Dear Aunty is quite well again unberufen & I hope will remain so – I am well but unfortunately rheumatism has settled in my right hip & it

[1] The Duchess of Edinburgh, the lively Russian-born wife of Affie, Prince Alfred the Duke of Edinburgh. Her daughter Victoria Melita later married Victoria's brother Ernie.

[2] Ernie was nearly thirteen, a rather feckless if lovable boy of whom the Queen sometimes almost despaired.

[3] The Queen deplored Victoria's occasional sharp tone in her writing as well as in her speech. She encouraged any sign of reform.

[4] Princess Victoria of Baden, subsequently mother-in-law of Victoria's daughter Louise.

prevents my walking for the last 10 days except very slowly – wh. annoys me dreadfully as in this weather I shd so like to walk a good deal.

Uncle Leopd. left us on Tuesday & is now at Claremont.

I am writing you a very stupid letter wh I am vexed at. Lady Erroll, Victoria Baillie & Miss Moore (a new Maid of Honour who I think you saw) are now here – & Sir H. Ponsonby, Sir J. McNeill, Capt. Bigge & Mr Sahl who arrived on Thursday. On the 31st we shall celebrate Halloween with torches etc & on the 1st we shall go again to the Glassalt Shiel.

Goodbye & God bless you dearest Child.

Ever your devoted Grandmama
V.R.I.

Love to all Have *you* got dear Gd.-Papa's Life[1] yourself? – Read my letter to Ella.

WINDSOR CASTLE
Dec 10 1881

Darling Victoria,

It is a long time since I wrote to you but I thank you for your last 2 dear letters of the 22nd & the 3rd Dec. I wish you to give this letter to dear Papa on the ever terrible 14th[2] when he & you will be going to pray in the dear last Resting place of those we loved & love so much.

Uncle Leopold has returned well & happy & we hear the nicest accounts of your future Aunt[3] who you have already had the pleasure of seeing – wh. I have not. Uncle Leopd. had several public engagements wh. are rather unfortunate just now when he ought to rest & be with us – It is also here raw & cold. Saturday mng. we had a little snow. Today it has rained & is very dark & foggy. On the 16th we hope to go to Osborne –

I hope you work regularly. Some knitting & plain work for the poor is such a nice occupation. *Only* reading is *not* good & work is such a good occupation for girls & women & it is such a pleasure to be able to be of use to others.

Auntie Beatrice is very well & much occupied for Christmas.

Love to all. Ever your devoted Mama [*sic*]
V.R.I.

---

[1] Theodore Martin's *Life of the Prince Consort*. Victoria required none of her grandmother's encouragement to read. She was a voracious reader all her life.

[2] A doubly 'terrible 14th' since the death of Princess Alice on the same day as that of her father.

[3] See footnote 1, page 2.

OSBORNE

Jan 25 1883
[wrongly dated for 1882]

Darling Victoria,

Many thanks for your last dear letter of the [?],[1] I am so glad to hear you are going to Arolsen wh. I am sure will be a great pleasure to you & to Uncle Leopold – We went over to Bagshot on Saturday & saw Aunt Louischen looking very well & the dear little Baby[2] wh is a nice little thing with a marked nose.

In looking over dear Mama's letters I found this touching passage wh. I shall certainly never forget; show it to dear Papa. I hope you will write to me abt. Arolsen & Helen. I fear Uncle Leopd. will be (as everyone is under those circumstances) very tiresome if he is absorbed with his Bride.[3] Tell me also if you have seen Sohn's[4] picture & how you like it.

We have a little frost now every night but it is off in the mng. & unfortunately the weather has become very foggy.

Now with many loves to all

Ever your devoted Mama [*sic*]
V.R.I.

What maid will come with you & later with Ella & Irène?

The Queen had begun this year the first of many early spring holidays in the south of France, a practice which Brown, a born xenophobe, deeply deplored. (Foreigners, besides being foreign, were given to laughing at his kilt.) Later, Victoria stayed with the Queen and would go for long drives in an open landau with her. She expressed astonishment at her grandmother's uncharacteristic distribution of largesse to the local children who followed eagerly behind crying 'Madame la Reine!'

[1] Evidently the Queen intended to insert the date later but forgot to do so.
[2] Princess Margaret of Connaught, born 15 January 1882.
[3] The Queen was invariably distressed, depressed and embarrassed at manifestations of affection between betrothed couples and avoided them whenever possible.
[4] Carl Sohn, the eminent painter.

CHALET DES ROSIERS, MENTONE
March 21 1882

Darling Victoria,

Many affte. loving thanks for your 2 dear letters of the 3rd & 13th
wh. gave me great pleasure. The attempt[1] of the 2nd was indeed a most
painful event but the affection & enthusiastic loyalty it has called forth
is very gratifying & soothing. Also from every single country there has
been such very great sympathy & kindness shown.

We left Aunt Louischen much better & I trust that she will soon get
much stronger & able to walk a little wh she has begun to do the last
few days. The little Baby is a gt. darling – & such a pretty little thing
with such fine large eyes & such a pretty little mouth & is so good.
Uncle Leopd. arrived here on Sunday. Our journey was very broilingly
hot, but beautiful from Marseilles especially from just before *Cannes* wh.
is lovely. The masses of Olives wh. abound all along here & the
orchards & orchards – laden with lemons – & also orange trees growing
half up the fine, high mountains – are quite marvellous, then Palm trees,
eucalyptus as high as elms & heliotrope & roses & every sort of lovely
rare plant – aloes – in number – prickly pear (a sort of cactus – *not* pretty)
in the gardens make the vegetation quite wonderful to see. Over all this
a deep blue sky & the calm sea from wh. you have delicious breezes &
you can well imagine the enchantment of the whole country, tho' the
sun is too hot to walk in except quite early in the mng. We have taken
some beautiful drives in the cool of the afternoon & eveng.

You have to put on a good thick shawl or cloak when the sun sets –
but that really is the only precaution necessary except for Invalids. The
nights are lovely. We have twice driven along the beautiful *Corniche*
road – on Saturday *into* Italy – & yesterday in the other direction to
beyond & above Monaco – most beautiful, a gt. height above the sea.
It was glorious & there was a splendid afterglow Alpenglühen on the
mountains behind.

I am sorry & surprised little fat Camilla[2] is going to be married. Who
have you got to replace her. Mary & the new French one may certainly
come with the others to Balmoral but who will be with you then? I
suppose Joey[3]?

I am glad you are going for Vicky's confirmation to Berlin but I
doubt your liking the place. Tell me what you think.

Poor Aunt Vicky has been *very* unwell & suffering & I only hope

[1] The seventh assassination attempt of her reign. A lunatic had shot at
her carriage outside Windsor station.

[2] Victoria's personal maid.

[3] Joey Rollstone, nursemaid to the Hesse children.

none of you will get ill – as I think the House is not very healthy. Aunt Vicky nearly had erysipelas & Aunt Lenchen[1] brought a dreadful throat back wh. she cld. not get rid of & wh. the Dr. here said was a *throat from bad drains.*[2]

Do tell Papa to be *very careful* abt. it. Let him see this letter & Ella too – & read out the descriptions to the others & tell Miss Jackson abt. Aunt Louischen & little Margaret.

Ever your devoted Grandmama
V.R.I.

It will indeed be [a] gt. pleasure to see you & dear Papa next month. I suppose Wilhelmina comes with you. The house is a nice little quiet Chalet surrounded by a Wood of Olives with Orchards of lemons under it & up above it – a beautiful view of the sea & coast *to the left* towards Bordighiera.

WINDSOR CASTLE
June 29 1882

Darling Victoria,

Not knowing if dear Papa has returned I enclose this letter to you for him. *You* will be looking forward to next Thursday & we are very sad at the prospect of losing the dear Sisters who are quite (as you were too) Kinder von Haus – & it is very sad for us & we shall miss them sadly – Auntie in particular – as they played & drew & read & worked together. Ella is not very strong & will require care & you *must not* expect her to do what *you* can; not long rides on rough horses etc.[3] And she must take plenty of milk & good meat etc. She is less strong than she was these 2 last years & has grown a gt. deal. Irène is a dear, good child

[1] Royal nicknames were sometimes given to avoid confusion between people of the same name, but sometimes they almost defeated their purpose. For 'Louischen' see footnote 1, page 16. 'Lenchen' was 'Louischen's' sister-in-law, Princess Helena, the Queen's fifth child, married since 1866 to Prince Christian of Schleswig-Holstein.

[2] The bad drains to which the Queen is referring were those in the Schloss at Berlin. Princess Helena had been staying there with the Crown Princess of Prussia and in her Journal entry for 18 March 1882 the Queen writes: 'Poor Vicky has been so unwell for a fortnight with an inflamed face and eye, and terrible neuralgia. She could hardly write excepting with a pencil. I canno' help feeling that their palace at Berlin is very unhealthy. Lenchen has returned from there with a bad ulcerated throat, and little Mossy had diphtheria ir December.'

[3] A Royal 'dig' at Victoria's continued practice of riding men's horses fo: several hours, of which the Queen strongly disapproved.

who got on extremely well here. She only dined twice a week with us. This afternoon she is going out alone with me as the others are still in London after the Concert.

Uncle Leopd. & Aunt Helen (except today) are here.

Ever your devoted Grandmama

V.R.I.

Many loves to Ernie & Alicky

The Queen was beset by numerous anxieties in 1882. On top of the Irish troubles, the situation in Egypt reached a crisis with the rebellion of Arabi Pasha, the Foreign Minister, against the Khedive. The Forts at Alexandria were bombarded by the Royal Navy on 11 July and Arabi was defeated by the troops of General Wolsley at Tel-el-Kebir. The Queen was proud of her son Arthur's modest contribution. Victoria's future husband, Prince Louis of Battenberg, was in action during the closing stages of the campaign.

OSBORNE

Aug 2 1882

Darling Victoria,

It is I fear long since I wrote – but I have been so busy & am still so, & so anxious especially as dear Uncle Arthur is gone with the Troops wh. is a trial to me. The parting was *agony*, for he has always been so dear, so very dear to me – & so good & so dutiful & unselfish & ever ready to do all I wished. May God bless & protect him. I don't think it will last long & I *hope* there won't be much fighting.

Many thanks for your 2 dear letters of the 10th & 28th. Rather long between. Bäuerlein arrived all right & well.

Poor Aunt Louischen is here with her beautiful Baby[1] *such* a darling – so good & friendly. It is a comfort having them with me now – & for Aunt also. Uncle Leopd. & Auntie Helen came on the 31st & had a gd. reception at E. Cowes – Uncle L. is not quite well & can't leave his room since the mng. after he arrived. I must end with many many loves

Ever Your devoted Grandmama

V.R.I.

Many kisses to the others.

[1] Princess Margaret ('Daisy') of Connaught, who married Prince Gustav Adolf of Sweden. He became King in 1950 and outlived his first wife by fifty-three years, dying at ninety-one in 1973. As a widower, he married for the second time Victoria's second daughter, Louise, in 1923.

OSBORNE

Aug 16 1882

Darling Victoria,

Many thanks for your last dear letters including the one of the 12th.

We have good accts. by letter from Malta & by Tel. from Alexandria of darling Uncle Arthur who is quite well & finds it quite cool. He landed his Brigade on Saturday & encamped at Ramleh (you shld. look at the Map – or shld I send you one?) where they at present remain – We hear Sir G. Wolsley arrived last night & Sir E. Wood at the same time.

I send Papa here a very *confidential* Dispatch from Sir A. Alison wh. he must not show to anyone & if possible send back by the next messenger. We have been on board 2 Transports & saw 3 sail; we saw many poor horses & mules on board.

The Confirmation of Eddie & George went off extremely well – only the heat was dreadful – But poor Uncle Leopd. has been in bed ever since. He had just got nearly well on the 5th & begun at once to do too much. On the evng. of the 8th he got a relapse & has (tho' not since the day before yesterday in the night) had a gt. deal of pain. Poor At. Helen is most devoted & we can hardly get her to leave him to get out.

Sophie & Mossy[1] are well & very good. Our splendid weather ever since the 26th has been succeeded by very showery days wh I hope won't go on. In gt. haste.

Ever your devoted Grandmama

V.R.I.

Love to the others. You shall hear abt. Cettawayo [*sic*][2] another day.

OSBORNE

Aug 25 1882

Dearest Victoria,

I write to you again today to enclose a letter for Miss Jackson & a copy of a letter from Sir J. McNeill wh. will interest Papa & all of you.

*We* can think of nothing but the events of this War.

Uncle Arthur telegraphs he has marched into Ismailia today. So far every thing progresses very well & our success on the Canal has been great – but *now* the difficulties will begin! It makes one so anxious –

You are going to the Manoeuvres & I know you always take so well what I tell you for your good & what I know dear Mama wished. I therefore hope you will *ride as little* as you *can* there. Drive as much as you like.

[1] Princess Margaret of Prussia, aged ten.
[2] Cetawayo, the Zulu chieftain, visited England in 1882.

Without a mother, & except for a Parade, or vorbei marsch[1] – or when you can be *entirely* under Papa's eye – it is not the place for a young unmarried Prss. & as Papa listens so much to what you say, if *you* tell him you feel yourself it is better *not* to ride then he will himself agree.

I wrote to him about it & *he* knows what I have always thought. For Ella it wld be bad for her health as well but then she *cannot* as Miss Jackson writes – ride just now. Dear Mama[2] ruined her health with those long rides on large rough horses. Uncle Leopd. is rather better but still on his sofa & I don't know when he will be able to move.

We have very stormy showery weather & to our gt. sorrow 3 of our poor men of the V. & Albert[3] were drowned the day before yesterday by the upsetting of a boat. It is dreadful.

We shall probably leave this [*sic*] on the 29th for Balmoral. How sad is the death of poor little Marie Polyxene of Hesse.[4]

Ever your devoted Mama [*sic*]

V.R.I.

BALMORAL CASTLE

Sept 5 1882

Darling Victoria,

I recd. your dear letter of the 27th Aug before we left Osborne & thank you much for it & for the *full* explanation abt. the Manoeuvres & your riding at it [*sic*]. I quite share your feelings abt. War & shedding blood – but we were driven into this – & as every thing in this world more or less – is the *sacrifice* of *few* for the *benefit* & *safety* of *many* – we can but hope & think that this War, wh. *cannot* be a long one will be of great use – & we are expecting to hear some great news very soon.[5]

Beloved Uncle Arthur – the flower of my sons – & my darling from his birth – is unberufen vy. well.

We hear often by telegraph & letters wh come slow [*sic*] & irregularly have begun arriving.

Aunt Louischen & Baby who is the greatest possible darling – are with us – & quite well & Uncle Leopd. is much better & able to embark

---

[1] March Past.

[2] The Queen, as always, is referring to Victoria's late mother.

[3] The Royal Yacht, *Victoria and Albert*.

[4] Princess Mary Polyxene of Hesse-Cassel, daughter of Prince Frederick William, died 16 August 1882.

[5] The battle of Tel-el-Kebir had taken place forty-eight hours earlier. It is likely that the Queen had already received a preliminary telegram.

tomorrow & comes round here by sea. At. Helen was most devoted during his illness.

I must end with many loves. People here ask after you 3 very much.
Ever your devoted Grandmama
V.R.I.

By the beginning of 1883 the Queen had given much thought to the marriage prospects of the four Hessian girls. 'Russia,' as she lays down firmly in this letter, 'I cd not wish for any of you.' In spite of her oft-repeated protestations that she was not a match-maker, it is evident in her letters to Victoria (and to numerous other of her relatives) that she experienced great satisfaction in planning advantageous marriages for Europe's numerous Royal children. More than that, she regarded it as a duty which none but she could perform. In the following letter she is already laying the foundations for a marriage between the second of the Hessian Princesses and Prince Frederick of Baden. But, clever, percipient and accomplished as she was, it is a sad fact that Queen Victoria's matchmaking plans were rarely fulfilled; and when they were often proved disastrous. A match with Fritz of Baden would per-haps have proved happier than the one Ella finally made.

OSBORNE
Jan 1 1883

Darling Victoria,

Many affte. thanks for your dear letter of the 27th & let me wish you all possible happiness in this New Year.

It is always a very serious thing to bid goodbye to the old one with all its anxieties, trials, sorrows & joys, & to look forward to *what* is un-known & to what *may* happen before this day comes round again.

But we must trust & rely on God's merciful protection & help – & the more we do that the more easily shall we be prepared to meet all the trials of this very uncertain world. Always think of that, dear Child – & you will find Life far more real & far easier.

I am glad you are going to Berlin. Do tell me what you think abt. Ella & Fritz of Baden? He is excellent? & I hear from all sides did his work admirably & with great selbst ständigkeit.[1] Ella shd not marry for

[1] Independence.

a year or 2 – but it wd. be a vy. nice & comfortable position for her. Russia, I cd. not wish for any of you & dear Mama always said she wd never hear of it. When shall we meet again? The Season is not a good time for you – & especially not for Ella – Do you think Irène & Alicky cd come together to Scotland or better not together? I consult you as I know dear Papa talks to you about all these things. How I shd like to see Papa trying to blow the Pipes.[1] He must bring them with him when he next comes over & get Ross or Campbell to give him a lesson.

It is wrong that the people at Darmstadt dislike his coming here.[2] Really he is never here more than 3 weeks or a month at a time & this last year was a great exception. Let me know what dresses you are going to wear at the Fancy [Dress] Ball.

I hope you go on with your modelling? Is Louis Battenberg quite well again?[3] How are the dogs?

Now with many loves & good wishes to the others –

Ever your devoted Grandmama

V.R.I.

The situation in Ireland had deteriorated even further. Charles Parnell, the Irish 'Home Ruler' and uncrowned 'king of Ireland', had been sent to jail in October 1881. He was released on 2 May 1882, Prime Minister Gladstone's 'most fatal move', commented the Queen. And she was right, too. On 4 May 1882, the newly appointed Irish Secretary, Lord Frederick Cavendish, was knifed to death in Phoenix Park, Dublin. His Under-Secretary, Charles Burke, died with him.

*The Times'* report of 12 February to which the Queen refers begins: 'Rumours of the most exciting character were in circulation for the last 48 hours respecting the evidence to be produced to-day in the Crown prosecution for the murder conspiracy. It was currently reported that . . . the final deliberations by which

[1] The Grand Duke had been given a set of bagpipes by the Queen as a Christmas present. Ross and Campbell were notable exponents of this instrument at Balmoral.

[2] The Court and senior citizens at Darmstadt resented the amount of time the Grand Ducal family spent in Britain. Princess Alice had been especially sensitive about this; her widowed husband was less so.

[3] The love between Princess Victoria and Prince Louis of Battenberg was fast ripening, and they became engaged on 1 July 1883.

the tragedy was arranged and the executioner appointed would be detailed by an eye-witness, that the principal assassins would be pointed out, and that the highest in social rank of the prisoners would be proved to have been on the ground at the time . . .'

Feb 21 1883

Darling Victoria,

I send you another letter abt. Aunt Louise wh. please after Papa & the others have seen, send on to At. Vicky.

I have to thank you for 5 dear letters wh. I certainly meant to answer long ago. Your dear letters always give me such pleasure as they contain so much. The little sketch of the Bulgarian Costume is so nicely done & I thank you so much for the pretty plate wh. is very nicely done.

We are here *quite absorbed* by the horrible disclosures in Dublin & you shd. get Miss Jackson to read the examination to you in The Times or Standard wh.ever you have got – beginning on the 12th & the accts. in the papers of the 17th & 19th are the most startling.

They fear that the originators are of a far higher class than those ordinary assassinators and that even Members of Parlt may be implicated!! It is too awful!

I send you some of little Baby Arthur's[1] Christening cake for all of you. I hope all will go off well at Berlin & that you will write to me about it all. How long do you stay? You will see Uncle Bertie & Uncle Affie & Auntie Marie.

I am sorry I can't write more today. But I am very busy. Uncle Leopd. & Aunt Helen who are staying here send many loves. Give mine to the Geschwistern.

Ever your devoted Mama [*sic*]

V.R.I.

Pss. Waldeck is also here.[2]

Ella, Princess Elizabeth of Hesse, was considered by many of her contemporaries as the loveliest of all young Princesses. But, in

[1] Prince Arthur of Connaught, born 13 January. He married Alix, Duchess of Fife, in 1913.

[2] Princess Helen, mother of the Duchess of Albany.

common with her youngest sister Alicky, she had a brooding, contemplative and even mystical streak in her character, which was susceptible to the attractions of the steppes, the dark interminable birch forests and the long cold winters of Russia. The frequent visits of the Russian Imperial family to Hesse, so deeply feared and deplored by the Queen, had taken their toll. Lovely Ella fell in love with the Grand Duke Serge, aged twenty-five.

The childless marriage ended in tragedy in 1905 when the Grand Duke, a notorious reactionary, was assassinated in Moscow. Ella subsequently dedicated her life to good religious works and founded the first and only religious nursing order in Russia, the Convent of Martha and Mary.

In July 1918 'Saint Elizabeth' was transported to Ekatarinburg with the Imperial family. After Tsar Nicholas and Ella's sister Alicky, their four girls and only son had all been gunned to death, Ella herself and other Romanoffs were taken to a mine-shaft and forced to leap down. Hand grenades were thrown after them by communist soldiers. Some survived the holocaust, and it was later discovered that, before she had died, she had succeeded in binding the wounds of some of her companions lying about her in the darkness.

Victoria subsequently wrote of the death of her next younger sister: 'If ever any one has met death without fear she will have & her deep & pure faith will have upheld & supported & comforted her in all she has gone through so that the misery poor Alicky will have suffered will not have touched Ella's soul.'[1]

BUCKINGHAM PALACE

March 7 1883

Dearest Victoria,

Pray tell dear Papa I could not write today but hope to do so tomorrow.

Oh! dear! How very unfortunate it is of Ella to refuse good Fritz of Baden so good & steady, with such a safe, happy position, & *for a Russian*. I do deeply regret it.

Ella's health will *never* stand the climate wh. killed your poor Aunt[2] &

[1] Princess Victoria of Hesse, by then Marchioness of Milford Haven, in a letter to her Lady-in-Waiting, Nona Crichton, 10 November 1918.

[2] Great-Aunt Marie, Princess of Hesse, wife of Emperor Alexander II of Russia. The Empress had died three years earlier at the age of fifty-six.

has ruined the healths of almost all the German Psses. who went there; besides the dreadful state Russia is in, & the very depressed bad state of Society. You told me, only quite lately darling Child, that you thought Ella cared for no one? What does this all mean?

It will give poor Papa much trouble & annoyance but I am doing all I can to make it smooth with the Empress who is badly annoyed.[1] What *does* Miss Jackson say?

Many thanks for your dear amusing letter of the 2nd – Do try & make some sketches of your costumes.

We have dreadfully cold weather – We are just returning to Windsor. Uncle Leopold's Baby[2] is a beautiful Child.

Ever your devoted Mama [*sic*]<br>V.R.I.

WINDSOR CASTLE

Ap 3 1883

Darling Victoria,

You will forgive & understand if I only write 3 words to wish you many, many happy returns of your dear birthday & to hope you will like the pearls & picture. But I am in such terrible distress at the loss not only of my best & most faithful attendant[3] but at the loss of my *dearest* & *best* friend – whom I had known for 34 years – & who for 18 years & ½ *never* left me for a day – that I cannot write of anything else. Love to all.

Ever your devoted Grandmama<br>V.R.I.

Prince Louis of Battenberg's next younger brother, and Victoria's future brother-in-law, Prince Alexander ('Sandro') of Battenberg, had taken on the thankless task of governing the northern half of Bulgaria as Sovereign Prince. At first he had

---

[1] The German Empress was indeed upset at Ella's refusal of the hand of Fritz of Baden and 'cut her dead' at a ball soon after the news became known. '. . . this unfortunate affair,' commented the Queen in her next letter (8 March 1883). 'The Empress seems very angry – she and the Badens had made *sure* of it – unwisely.'

[2] Princess Alice of Albany, later Countess of Athlone.

[3] John Brown had just died. The Queen was to feel his loss deeply and for long.

enjoyed Russian support, but when his uncle, Tsar Alexander II died, and was succeeded by Sandro's hostile cousin Alexander III, his task became a misery and he was no more than a pawn in the political machinations of Germany and Russia, and the subject of much sympathy from Queen Victoria.

The Queen had first met Sandro and his brother Louis at Balmoral four years earlier. She confided in her Journal that Sandro 'is not very like his brother, much taller, 6 foot 2¾, dark, more like his mother, broad, & with a very good figure, a very open, good-natured face, good looking, but hardly as much as his brother Louis, who is 3 years older. . . . Both Sandro & Louis are so amiable intelligent, & nice, so well brought up.'


OSBORNE

May 2 1883

Darling Victoria,

I cld not manage to write by the messenger but do so now – to thank you for your last dear letter of the 28 April. Your acct. of dear Sandro's difficulties grieve me, as I like him & pity him, & wish he cd get clear of Russia who is never to be trusted.

The death of your good Uncle of Schwerin[1] is much to be regretted & I feel much for dear Grandmama who has *lost* so many. Dear Papa feels it also, much.

Alas! As one goes on in life this must be – but *my* fate in *this* respect is *particularly* hard & sad. I am so *lonely* and since dear Grandpapa was taken have one by one lost *all* those who cld be a help & support to me – & this *one* of my *dear, devoted, faithful* attendant & *trust* [*sic*] friend Brown who looked after everything, anticipated every wish & whose help & support I miss *hourly* – & at every turn – has quite crushed me. I fear dear Ella will find it *very* different & very dull to be with us now! And poor Balmoral will be especially sad, nothing gay will be going on. Tell her that, with many thanks for her last 2 dear letters, so that she may not be disappointed.

An addition to our sorrows & troubles has occurred yesterday, in the death of the kind & good Dean of Windsor Mr Connor for many years my Chaplain & Vicar of Newport & an old, kind friend of ours.

I *think* Papa must have known him – Dear Mama did, I think. Poor Major Ewen's death was too sad. But I am glad to say his son has been

[1] Frederick Francis II, Grand Duke of Mecklenburg-Schwerin, who married the Grand Duke of Hesse's sister, Anna.

appointed Messenger. Uncle Leopold's Baby – dear little Alice[1] is here with us. She is such a pretty good child.

I rejoice to think that we shall see you & Irène with dear Papa D.V. at the beginning of Aug: I trust Irène may remain afterwards some little time with us wh. I am sure will be good for her & very pleasant for us. Thank him so much for his kind letter wh. I will answer very soon. My leg is getting on well.[2] Since the day before yesterday I can walk with 2 strong sticks in my rooms, but not up & down stairs; *that* won't be for some time.

Oh! the leg will get well but *not* the *sick heart*!

Dear Auntie has got the rheumatism in her right arm wh. prevents her writing! Uncle Leop^d & Aunt Helen are at Fontainebleau.

With many loves to the others

Ever your devoted Grandmama

V.R.I.

I hope you liked the Chalk head I sent you? How is your arm.


The Queen had taken no part in bringing about the engagement of Prince Louis of Battenberg to his first cousin's daughter, Princess Victoria, and the news came as a surprise – though not complete surprise – to her.

Victoria was desperately anxious to learn what her grandmother's views of the engagement might be, and she was never more relieved in all her life than when she read the following letter; although she was quite unable to reassure her on the question of 'the fortune'.

In fact, Louis and Victoria, although separated in age by nine years, had known one another since early childhood and had become engaged as if destined from their birth to a lifelong love affair – as indeed it turned out to be. In terms of their rank and the age in which they lived, they did not know wealth all their lives.

So much for Victoria's engagement. Ella's engagement was something entirely different, and at this time the Queen is quite refusing to accept its inevitability.

---

[1] Princess Alice of Albany.

[2] The Queen had fallen downstairs at Windsor on 17 March 1883. Rheumatic pains followed, which the Queen did not take lightly. It was an untimely moment for Brown to die.

BALMORAL CASTLE

June 19 1883

Darling Victoria,

I cannot be silent, when I have heard from dear Papa – & also through Ella that you *are almost* – or perhaps *are really* – engaged to Louis Battenberg.

You will I know be anxious to know what *I* think? I think that you have done well to choose only a Husband who is *quite* of your way of thinking & who in many respects is as English as you are – whose interests must be the same as yours & who dear Mama liked.

Besides you do *not* leave dear Papa who needs your help as much as the dear Geschwistern do. One only drawback I see – & that is 'the fortune'. *I* don't think *riches* make happiness, or that they are necessary, but I *do* think a certain amount is a necessity so as to be independent. And this I *hope* you will be able to reassure me upon – & have well thought of before you take the irrevocable step. I am rather sorry to hear from Papa that he speaks as if Ella's marriage was to be. Ella herself says 'There is no hurry' & that she *don't* wish to go to Russia & that *if* it was [word omitted] must be made for her living out of Russia. I think *you* shld. get Papa to make this an *absolute condition*, & *not* to hurry it on. Ella ought to be 20 before she marries.[1]

I am still very lame & suffer from neuralgic pains – My spirits are the same – & it is in short the constant missing of that merry buoyant 'nature' of my dearest Brown wh. depresses me so terribly & wh. makes everything so sad & joyless! – And this I carry everywhere about with me. He helped in so many things – more perhaps here than any where, that everything is filled with Wehmuth![2]

I must end for today hoping to hear from yourself about your prospects.

Ever your devoted Grandmama

V.R.I.

The Queen liked her grandchildren to visit her for as long as possible before they were married in order that she might have a last opportunity of advising them on the joys and problems of married life. In the Queen's mind these visits were of special importance and were in no way to be interfered with. She was

[1] She would be 20 on 1 November 1884. In fact, she married on 15 June of that year.
[2] Melancholy.

therefore very put out when it appeared that the intimate tranquillity with Victoria to which she had looked forward seemed to be threatened by the simultaneous appearance on the Isle of Wight of Victoria's father and her own noisy, gregarious son, Bertie, the Prince of Wales.

OSBORNE

July 29 1883

Darling Victoria,

I send these few lines by Mr Sahl who has begged to be allowed to go over & meet you – to thank you for your last kind letters & to say how grieved I am to be still so much of an Invalid & able to do so little. I fear altogether I shall be a very dull companion.

Louis Battenberg is coming here tomorrow & I shall be very pleased to see him. But I much regret that what I *told* Papa nearly a *month ago* has *not been listened to* & that he is coming to be at Cowes with Uncle Bertie, for I wished to have you to *myself*, & as you *are*, for the *last time* – how can I avoid asking him, & Uncle Bertie will be constantly wanting *you* to go to him. This *last* I do *protest against*.

I trust you will have a fine passage & Irène not be sick. You will just see Uncle Leopold & no more. It will indeed be a very *great* pleasure to see you all again, but everything is clouded over for *me* now!

I have very good accts. of dear Auntie who finds the Douches do her gt. good & likes the place. She is to be back on the 12th or 13th

Now auf wiedersehen.

Ever your devoted Grandmama<br>V.R.I.

Love to dear Papa & all.

The most endearing qualities of the Queen as a correspondent are all revealed in the following letter from Osborne in the late summer of 1883, a year which had been marked for the Queen by a number of incidents and occasions – her own injury and the death of Brown among them – which had darkened it with sadness.

Partings with those she loved always saddened her, and the last parting with Victoria before she was married and – in a sense – parted from her for ever, clearly affected her deeply. How movingly she writes of the Royal Yacht's silent night departure from the Isle of Wight with her grand-daughter on board!

The Queen had seen how dangerous it could be to question too closely the basic tenets of the Protestant faith. Like the Queen's eldest daughter, Vicky, Princess Alice had also for a time succumbed to 'the *side* of Science and Philosophy – as opposed to real faith'. Her little son's fall and death had changed all that, and led Alice back from the dangers of rationalism to what the Queen regarded as the true path.

In this letter, too, we read again of the Queen's dark distrust of 'M. House' – Marlborough House, the Prince of Wales's London establishment, and in the Queen's mind a baleful influence on the mind of a young girl.

Finally, in her reference to the letters of '*my* dear Grand Mother', we see the Queen as a conscientious editor who is offended by the smallest inaccuracy.


OSBORNE

Aug 22 1883

Darling Victoria,

Your dear little Note from Havre on board the OSBORNE gave me great pleasure. To take leave of you at night, & never to see you *again* (as I *fear* it will not be *possible* for me to go to your marriage) – as a dear girl, – as you are now, was very painful to me & I felt it terribly.

Every thing upsets me now & the heavy cloud which overhangs every thing causes partings to be more deeply felt than ever.

Its being at night too was particularly sad. I always hate 'goodbyes' at night or leaving any place at night. I saw the OSBORNE lit up gliding like a meteor over the Solent!

You are so good & sensible that I am sure you will be a steady good wife & *not* run after amusements, but find your happiness chiefly in your own home. Beware of London & M. Hse.

There is one thing wh. I had wished to speak to you abt. but had no opportunity of doing so, & that is: that I wld. *earnestly* warn you agst. trying to *find* out the *reason* for & explanation of *everything*.

Science can explain *many things*, but there is a spiritual as well as a material World & this former *cannot* be *explained*. We must have *faith* & *trust*, & believe in an all ruling, all wise & benificent Providence wh. orders all things. To try & find out the *reason* for everything is very dangerous & leads to nothing but disappointment & dissatisfaction, unsettling your mind & in the end making you miserable.

No one felt this more than dear Mama who felt *all* the blessedness & comfort of faith & trust wh. no philosophy can give after having for a time tested the other. Dear Grandpapa used to say: 'die Vernunft geht nur so weit und wo die Vernunft aufhört da muss der Glauben anfangen'.[1]

And so it is – Dear Aunt Vicky unfortunately has taken the *side* of Science & Philosophy – as opposed to real faith, whereas both should go *together* & I would earnestly warn you to avoid these topics with her – There is a beautiful Poem by Tennyson called 'In Memoriam' wh. I send you as I think you wld. like & admire it. Tell me how you like it when you have begun it. The copy I always read was given me by poor darling Mama.

I also send you this Life of dear Grand Papa in German wh. I wish to offer to Gustaf Erbach & have written into it. I have signed *Cousin* on acct. of our relationship.

The collection of letters of *my* dear Grand Mother (who was 1st Cousin to *his* father – he being my 2nd cousin once removed) is most interesting but I think it is a pity they left the faulty orthography. And some of the English names *shld.* be corrected – for that was merely as she did not catch them rightly.

When I get a few more copies I will correct the names in one, for I knew the people.

For instance there is Mr & Mrs Horace Sims or *Simms* wh. ought to be *Seymour*; as they were the Parents of Admiral Sir Beauchamp Seymour, the *hero* of Alexandria, now Ld. Alcester. My Governess was not called Leesen but *Lehzen*.

From Saturday the heat is quite intense! Little Alice misses you all & I am sure we do. This letter is so long I must end here & will write (if possible) to Ella tomorrow.

Ever your devoted loving Grandmama

V.R.I.

Love to all – & remembrance to Miss Jackson who I hope *will write*. Auntie sends many loves.



In Bulgaria political skulduggery had led to personal anguish and the breaking of two hearts. Like his brother Louis, Sandro had fallen in love with one of Queen Victoria's grand-daughters, in his case 'Cousin Vicky', Princess of Prussia, and second daughter of the Crown Prince and Princess, 'Aunt Vicky' and 'Uncle Fritz'. Politically, a marriage was out of the question, according to

---

[1] The Queen is quoting a saying of Prince Albert: 'Reason goes only so far, and where reason stops, belief must begin.'

Germany's 'Iron Chancellor', Prince Bismarck, who recognized
that it would give offence to Russia. He forbade it, to the chagrin
of Queen Victoria, and the distress of the lovers. However, at
the time the next letter was written, the Queen still held out
some hope of bringing the affair to a successful conclusion and
thus displeasing her special enemies, the Tsar and Bismarck.

As to the match between Ella and Grand Duke Serge which,
conversely, the Queen was conspiring to destroy, she was now
encouraged by the latest news that her words of wisdom and
warning to her grand-daughter had borne fruit. Having failed
with Fritz of Baden, she saw new hope in a Scandinavian match.

BALMORAL CASTLE

Aug 30 1883

Darling Victoria,

Tho' I wrote on Tuesday I must write again – This time it is about
Sandro. I think I told you at Osborne that Aunt Vicky feared Uncle
Fritz wld. make gt. difficulties. But I don't think I told you that Aunt V.
wrote to me that Victoria (to whom the *possibility* of Sandro's *wishing* to
marry *her* has *not* been told) is violently *in love* with Sandro; says she
never cared for anyone else, or ever *will* marry any one else; – that she
will wait any time for him & has refused to *look* at *any* other Princes
who might be good partis for her. Uncle F. was very angry & tried to
put it out of her head – but he did not succeed & she is more than ever
anxious abt. it. I got another letter from At. V this mng of wh. I send
you an extract. Now cld. you through Ludwig[1] manage to get Sandro
*not* to *come forward now* – & let *him* know of V's feelings so as to induce
him to wait possibly it *might* come to pass.

This must be done *very confidentially* & *secretly* –

I shall certainly not say a word to Ella abt. Pce Charles of Sweden –
but I must say I rejoice that she has acted as she has done abt. Serge, for
I own I *dreaded* this marriage very much for *her*. Papa was quite right in
saying I did not set her *agst*. Serge but I did tell her to reflect well before
she accepted him & to remember the climate & the state of the Country
& that (contrary tó what she wished & wh: I had *thought* possible) her
*living* out of Russia cld only be the *exception* to the rule – I shall never
deny having said *this* for I think so. At. Marie is very wrong to call it an
insult when there was never any *serious* question of it – yet. I never gave
Ella credit for so much independence of character. Uncle Leop^d will
be delighted – but I won't mention Charles of Sweden to him.

[1] The Queen had referred earlier to Prince Louis as 'Louis', but, perhaps
recognizing the confusion with his future father-in-law, now usually referred
to him as 'Ludwig'.

Charlotte is doing wonders with my arm & leg – Our weather is not good.

The Russian family think it such an honour to marry any one of them – that a refusal appears to them so impossible as to be *insulting*.

Love to all. Ever your devoted Mama [*sic*]

V.R.I.

BALMORAL CASTLE

Sept 4 1883

Darling Victoria,

Aunt Vicky seems very anxious that dear Papa *shld know what* has passed abt. Vicky & Sandro as she (Aunt V.) *may* wish to speak to him abt. it. So will *you* tell him *all*?

I am rather distressed that Serge is after all coming. If only Ella remains firm? I *can't* tell you *how* I dread that marriage for her. *Believe me* it wld be *misery* for her as the climate, Society etc. are *pernicious* there – And darling Mama said again and again to me, nice as Serge was, she *never* wld. hear of one of her girls going there.

Ever your devoted Grandmama

V.R.I.

Young Vicky is quite fretting & miserable abt. Sandro! I got the Brochure abt. Kaspar Hauser[1] but no letter. *Who* sent it.

After first informing Victoria that it would be quite impossible for her to come to her wedding in Darmstadt, the Queen changed her mind, certainly out of affection for her grand-daughter, and also, perhaps, because she recognized that her presence would cement further the British court's very close relations with Hesse and undermine Russian influence, which she had long deplored and feared. If her presence, and her persuasion, should cause Ella finally to turn against Grand Duke Serge, so much – so *very* much – the better.

[1] The subject of a great *cause célèbre*, Kaspar Hauser was a German youth of mysterious origin who claimed to be heir to the throne of Baden. He died of a stab wound which, he claimed, was inflicted by a stranger but may have been self-inflicted.

BALMORAL CASTLE

Sept 11 1883

Darling Victoria,

I thank you so much for your dear letter of the 6th – all about Sandro. I am doing all I can to get the Govt. to support & help him. As for Ella, I am very uneasy & anxious lest *she* shld. be taken in – for Heaven & Earth will [be] moved to get hold of her – & with Ella's character & health I can see nothing worse than her living in Russia. Believe *me* *when* I speak so strongly agst. it.

Let me now tell you something wh. I have been thinking of very much since you left. I said I *feared* it wld. be impossible for me to be *present* at your dear marriage as the travelling abroad under such sadly altered circumstances wld be *so* painful. This is *quite true but* I have thought that I *might* be of *use* to you – & to dear Papa, as Grossmama is so far from well, & I have *also thought* that as some are *not* pleased at the marriage, *my* presence *wld.* be a support.

I have thought that the most unbearable & trying part of the travelling wld. be got over if I only went straight to Darmstadt – to your Palais, if Papa cld. lodge me for a week & went straight *back again.* If I look on this as a sacred duty to your darling Mama's eldest Child – whom she specially recommended to me; in one of her letters wh. will appear in the Life she says she wishes me to look on you, as on one of my own Children, *for that* one cld. not tell what might not happen! Only I must beg to be dispensed from appearing at any festivities of an Evng. etc & I shld. hope in that case nothing wld. be asked.

Unfortunately now I hear from Uncle Bertie that the marriage was to be in the 1st week of Feb: – Of course that wld. make it *impossible.* If it was Easter time *I might* manage it – if I am well enough – & I wld. for your dear sake & that of all you dear Children, dear Mama's & Papa's, make the painful effort. There is a satisfaction in sacrificing oneself to be of use to others.

We have a beautiful day & both Aunties are gone out with the 3 Cousins to Loch Callater. I went with dear Auntie Beatrice, Harriet Ph: & Amy Lambart[1] to the Glassalt for the day yesterday but it upset me dreadfully.

'Charlotte' has only 5 days more to finish her *massage* wh. I think will be most successful.

Love to all. I send a handkerchief I bought at the merchant's[2] for Ernie.

Ever your devoted Grandmama

V.R.I.

[1] Harriet Phipps and Amy Lambart were Maids of Honour to the Queen.
[2] The local shop near Balmoral.

Sept 21 1883

Darling Victoria,

I hasten to answer your dear letter of the 17th recd. yesterday. Both from that & from a letter from dear Papa I see that you appreciate the gt. effort I mean to try & make to be present at your Wedding & I know you will kindly help me in making things as quiet as possible for me.

Dear Papa says that according to German custom wh. was like the English, marriages do *not* take place in Lent. I did *not* know that this was always the case in Germany. Tell him that in England it was merely a fashion of late years, & that it is going off now again, as many people one knows have been married in Lent, last & this year.

However any way there wld have been no question of my going there except about Easter time. I wld like to arrive *in* Passion Week, so as to have a few quiet days alone with you all, & the Wedding cld. be any time after that, wh. suited.

The Visitors *whoever* they are I hope wld only be asked for 2 or 3 or 4 days. I *like quiet abroad*. And this next year it will be very trying to me in every way.

As regards Ella I quite understand what you say. But there is one subject you have not touched upon wh. I consider as great a danger as *any* – that is the *very bad state* of Society & its *total want of principle*, from the *Grand Dukes downwards* – wh. Ludwig & Sandro know well. Serge & Paul[1] are exceptions but I hear the former is not improved of late. And I fear our sweet but *undecided* & *inexperienced* Ella, with her lovely face, may be misled & get into difficulties & troubles – wh. might have painful consequences.

Louis will understand what I mean. Russians are *so* unscrupulous.

You say that if the idea shld. be entertained, Ella wld insist on spending a good part of every year out of Russia. If she *can* get this promise given & above all, kept, right & well – but she must *not* look to being *much* & *often* with *me* – as I cld. *not* have a *Russian Gd. Duke* staying with *me often* or *for long* – That wld be *utterly impossible* & I wish dear Ella shld look at all the difficulties & drawbacks until she embarks in what afterwards she might *regret*.

With you & Louis the case is totally different, you are both *my* subjects – Louis in my Service, & you will be at Home in England & with me at any time.

*Politics* or *no* politics the Russians are *totally* antagonistic to England. I entrust all these things to you.

[1] Serge's brother, Grand Duke Paul, who married Princess Alexandra of Greece. She died two years later and Paul was assassinated in 1919.

*Two* very *private* little *observations* I must make.

1. I *beg* Papa & you *not* to hint *as yet* abt. my coming to Uncle Bertie or At. Vicky. Dear Uncle cannot keep anything to himself – but lets everything *out* – & At. V. wld. at once insist on coming at the beginning & staying all the time wh. I *most particularly* wish her *not* to *do*. I had experience of this at Coburg, when I had constantly to have to *avoid* perpetual visits to breakfast etc. Besides she & Uncle F. are *not* pleasant in *Germany*. They are high & mighty there.[1] So *I beg* they might be asked for a very *short time* & Uncle B. & Aunt Alix too; – but they [Vicky and Fritz] are *very discreet*. Please explain this all to dear Papa, & ask him to say that for various reasons – the time of year etc – the marriage wld probably not be *till after Easter*.

I must end this long letter.

Ever your devoted Grandmama
V.R.I.

Tell Louis *not* to mention it yet to *his* Parents *either*. Give him my love, I am glad Sandro has given back the Constitution, bad tho' it is.


The frequent vacillations of Ella's heart exhausted everyone, and particularly the Queen who, at last, in October 1883, is beginning to accept the final inevitability of Ella's 'going to terrible Russia'. But she remains agonized and quite unreconciled to the prospect.


BALMORAL CASTLE
Oct 21 1883

Darling Victoria,

I have not yet thanked you for your last dear letter of the 6th – but am glad that the difficulties wh. dear Papa apprehended have been got over. I have got Ella's letter but I *really* do *not* feel *quite* able to answer her *yet* – as I *do* feel this prospect *so very deeply*. I *know how* dearest Mama was *agst*. the idea, (tho' *personally* she liked Serge) & I also feel that Ella will be *quite lost to me* for a Russian Gd. duke is a *person* belonging to Russia, & Russia is *our real enemy* & totally antagonistic to *England*.

This is *very painful* for you know *how* dear you are to me – how like my own Children – & that therefore it is a great wrench & trial to me. It may be that Serge will get out of that very exclusive Panslavist Regt. & I hope dear Papa will *insist* on the marriage *not* taking place *till* Ella

---

[1] Queen Victoria could not endure the stuffy superiority of the Prussian court. She found even her eldest daughter difficult to deal with in Germany.

is 20 or *nearly* so – & on *their* living a good part of the year *out* of *Russia*. I also hope I may still see a *little* of her once more, before she marries – *without* the *Intended* (for I suppose he will be by this time) as I have a *particular* aversion to being mixed up with Brautstand[1] – & I hope I may be spared *that*.

Pray *beg* Papa *not* to have him at Darmstadt when I am *there*; it wld *spoil every*thing for *me* –

Dear Ella, she is really being changeable & *unaccountable*; she told me how she hated the Russians, she refused Serge 3 weeks ago & now she takes him & forgets *all*!! I own, I think dear Irène is right when, quite naïvely, à propos of Ella's *not* taking Fritz of B. wh. I said I regretted as I thought she wld. not easily find so good a person – (tho' I never blamed her refusing him if she did not care for him) – she said, 'Oh! I think she wld be happy with anybody!' Pray don't let poor Irène hear this.

I said to Papa (whom I wrote to 2 days ago & he will very likely show you my letter) that whatever I felt I did not intend to follow the example of certain people's behaviour with respect to F. of B. when Ella refused him. – *You* may tell Ella what I feel & that in a few days I will write to her.

The Russians' behaviour towards Sandro is *monstrous* –

Irène tells you all we do – so I don't say anything abt. that. Later I must speak to you abt. my visit to Darmstadt & the rooms & people. *I cld. not sleep* in dearest Mama's Bedroom – tho' I wld. gladly sit there – or dress there – I had better send my own Bed wh. I always take with me –

Now goodbye darling Child, here is some *white* heather from the Glassalt wh. Campbell dried & gave me & wh. I said I wld send you.

Ever your devoted Mama [*sic*]<br>V.R.I.

WINDSOR CASTLE
Nov 28 1883

Darling Victoria,

I thank you very much for your dear letters of the 1st & the 22nd. I hope you will ask Ella to show you the letter I have written her. The Verlobung[2] is now a fact & Serge *is* nice[3] & seems so devoted to her,

---

[1] State of being betrothed. (See footnote 3, page 35.)

[2] Engagement.

[3] This judgement was based on hearsay as she did not meet him for another six months. When she did so she found him congenial if very delicate.

that *if* the *conditions* of spending a good time *every* year *out of Russia* & of the marriage *not* being till she is nearly 20 – I *trust* it may turn out happily. What I say to Ella abt. marriage *in general*, I wld wish also to say to *you*; for it is very necessary to look on it in a *serious light*. So many girls think to marry is *merely* to be independent & amuse oneself – whereas it is the very *reverse* of independence – 2 wills have to be *made* to act together & it is *only* by *mutual* agreement & *mutual yielding* to one another that a happy marriage can be arrived at. I hope *you* will go away for a day or 2 after your marriage (I mean the same day) to Kranichstein or Jugenheim, as dear Mama & Papa did & Uncle Affie & At. Marie did to Zarsko for 2 days. It wld be so much nicer – Then I wish to know if *Trains* are to be worn *at* the Ceremony or not?

Dear Irène is such a dear, good child, so unselfish & good tempered & always pleased & very *sensible* & so affectionate. We shall be so sorry to lose her.

Hoping you are all well,

Ever your devoted Grandmama

VRI

The responsibility of having such a grandmother to her wedding was a heavy one, as Victoria was beginning to learn; although she would not know just how onerous until later. The Queen's visit to Darmstadt was complicated by the fact that her health appeared to be very precarious. Almost as serious was the ill-health of one of her dogs.

OSBORNE

*Jan 21 1884*

Darling Victoria,

So many thanks for your last dear letter of the 29th Dec – Since then we have again had a visit from Louis Battenberg who was very well and cheerful.

Lily of Hanover[1] spent a week with us & left on Saturday & Aunt Lenchen was here for 3 nights & left this mng.

I am sorry poor Irène is so plagued with her teeth. Why did she not follow the directions of Mr Fairbank who is a very good dentist?

Auntie [Beatrice] has sent you a Mem^d abt our coming & I hope I shall not be giving much trouble. I am however still a very poor creature. I can hardly stand at all – & must be led down stairs, – I can

[1] Princess Frederica of Hanover.

go up stairs by holding on by the bannisters or a rope agnst the wall, & I must be led & helped in & out of a carriage by my own Servant.

Dear beautiful Noble has been very poorly for the last few days with an upset stomach & incapacity of eating tho' he has eaten again – but as he is old, it made me very anxious & still does. He is so dear & good & sensible – I know how you all loved him – & then dear Brown was so fond of him!

It is more than 3 weeks since I had a letter from you! I suppose you write a gt. deal to Louis Battenberg?[1]

I must end rather in a hurry

Ever your devoted Mama [*sic*]
V.R.I.

OSBORNE

Feb 13 1884

Darling Victoria,

I was a little startled by the news recd. in your dear letter of the 11th recd. this mng as to the change of day but the 16th will suit me equally well. D.V. we hope to be with you on the 10th or 9th Ap. But what will be done abt. all the Fêtes? It will *never* do that you are *not* present at any & you *must* have 2 quiet days at Jugenheim[2] 17th & 18th. Ludwig is *very* strong abt. this & so am I. You cld. return for any Fetes on 19th 21st 22nd surely & then go back to Jugenheim – We cld stay till the 24*th*.

Tell dear Papa that the Empress A. is very anxious I shld. see the Empr. at Darmstadt – (is he coming from Wiesbaden) & not at *Coblentz* where I wld *go one* day to see the Empress from Darmstadt, coming back the same day; Would Papa allow that? Only a mng. visit.

Pray answer upon all these points *as soon as possible*. Westerweller[3] is again pressing for the List of evy. body & I am so afraid he will do – as last time – upset Papa's arrangements.

I must end for today to save the Post

Ever your devoted Grandmama
V.R.I.

[1] She did.
[2] The village above which Schloss Heiligenberg was situated.
[3] Major-General P. Westerweller, Chamberlain to the Grand Duke of Hesse.

Prince Leopold, Duke of Albany, the Queen's haemophilic son, died on 28 March 1884 at Cannes after yet another fall. He is often referred to as the nicest and most innocently fun-loving of all Queen Victoria's sons. He was certainly the most loved by Victoria and her sisters. Like most haemophiliacs, he was doted on by his protecting mother, and Queen Victoria felt his loss dreadfully, just as all mothers can suffer worst from the death of a disabled child. Leopold's body was brought back to England and buried at Windsor. His tomb is in the Albert Memorial Chapel.

'Uncle Leo' died within a few hours of John Brown's death a year earlier, a coincidence which the Queen noted with fatalistic satisfaction.

The tragedy led to the postponement of Victoria's wedding.


WINDSOR CASTLE
Ap 2 1884

Darling Victoria,
    Your dear sad letter of the 29th touched me much! *I* knew what *you* wld feel & what wld be the loss of beloved 'Uncle Leo' to you & dear Papa! The whole Country as well as we ourselves are in deepest mourning – There is such sorrow! Darling Uncle was so beloved, people thought him so like his precious father, that he was following in His footsteps, that he wld [be] (& he was) a gt. help to me – & *now* – *all, all* is ended & He is with Him & darling Mama!! free from all his constant sufferings & trials! This dear Helen herself feels & says! *Nothing* can exceed her goodness, patience, unmurmuring unselfish resignation. It is too touching to see her. We were at Claremont on Saturday & yesterday.

    On Friday the dear Remains arrive here – & *I* shall go to the Station South Western, with Aunties Lenchen & Beatrice (she feels it so dreadfully) & follow them up to the Albert Chapel – where they will remain till the last sad ceremony (when we shall be present). Poor dear Helen wishes very much to come over on Friday to go to the Albert Chapel – there to hear a prayer! I hope she may be able! You will be with us – all of you, in spirit & prayer I am sure! Papa will tell you how I long to come for a few days quiet to you all. I need it. Is it not extraordinary & awful that all this shld happen almost at the very moment as last year – & 4 hours only after my dearest best friend was taken *last year*! And these days are again days of mourning!

I am sorry it shld have to be on your dear birthday but it was un-avoidable.[1] What will be done abt your wedding?

Thank dear Ella & Irène for their touching letters for I have no time to write yet. 100ds & 100ds of telegrams & letters keep pouring in.

God bless you. Ever your devoted sorrowing **Grandmama**

V.R.I.

I am sure Ernie & Alicky are grieved.

WINDSOR CASTLE
April 10 1884.

Darling Victoria,

Two words to say that we intend D.V. to leave this [*sic*] on the 15th (Monday 14th is Easter Monday & a bad & almost dangerous[2] day for travelling) so hope weather permitting to arrive on Thursday 17th at 9.[3] Pray tell dear Papa that I beg to be *recd totally in private* & the carriage to be closed, *one* of my 2 Highland servants going on it – as I must be helped. They are both (as I said before) Upper servants now. I rejoice much to see you all & to be of some little use, besides I must have some complete rest. Otherwise travelling is very painful to me now. Bid dear Papa *not* to ask Aunt Vicky *before* the 25*th or* 26*th*.

I am very tired & very sad – & so is poor dear Auntie Beatrice. I thought Ernie & Alicky wld write to me.[4] Dear Uncle loved them, as he did you all, so much & Alicky was such a pet! I *hope* they feel what a loss He is to them too?

Many loves to all. Ever your devoted sorrowing **Grandmama**

V.R.I.

The widowed Grand Duke of Hesse had formed a liaison with the divorced wife of the Russian *chargé d'affaires* to the Hessian court, a Madame de Kolemine. As a mistress she was perfectly acceptable at Darmstadt, and everyone was relieved that the Grand Duke should find happiness and consolation in the woman.

Unfortunately, Victoria's father let it be known that he in-tended to *marry* his mistress. Queen Victoria, already in poor

[1] The Queen is referring to the Duke of Albany's funeral, 5 April 1884.

[2] Doubtless a reference to congestion and the difficulties of travel. *Plus ça change . . . !*

[3] Itinerary details were taken care of by the Queen's staff, but she never completely trusted them.

[4] Ernst-Ludwig was a reluctant letter-writer all through his life. Alicky was eleven years old.

physical shape and deeply distressed by the death of her son, was outraged at the news which filtered through to her soon after she had completed her arduous journey to Darmstadt.

NEUES PALAIS, DARMSTADT

Ap 26th 1884

Darling Victoria,

As you were charged by your dear Papa to make the painful communication to me of his intended marriage – asking me not to think ill of him & turn away from him, I think it best to repeat in writing what I said to you on the subject. – First of all, I shall never turn against or away from dear Papa – I know how attached he is to me and mine, I know how many excellent qualities he has – how happy he made dear Mama, how much she loved him & how much he loves you all – But it will make an immense difference between us. In England his remarrying *now*, before Irène is married (& she is much too young for that) and his marrying such a person – a divorced Russian Lady – would lower him so much that I cld. not have him near so much as before. – And I am sure it wld shock his Brothers & Sisters in Law (at least most of them) very much. I am sure if dear Uncle Leopold had been here he wld have spoken very strongly on this subject to him.

He cannot say that this intended union is for the sake of his Children or for his Country – it wld be the vy. reverse of *both*, it can only be for what *he thinks*, (& I am afraid he is much mistaken) will be for his *own* personal happiness. It will do him immense harm in his own Country – in England he will lose the position he held & enjoyed & *I* cld *not* defend such a choice.

If dear Papa should feel lonely when you 3 elder are married – I should say nothing (tho it must pain me) if he chose to make a morganatic marriage with some nice, quiet, sensible & amiable person – who would at any rate command the respect of us all as well as of his Country.

But to choose a Lady of another religion who has just been divorced – who no doubt has tried to obtain Papa's sympathy as well as admiration, wld I fear be a *terrible mistake* & one which he wld soon repent of, when *too late*.

The Lady wld be in such a disagreeable position that she wld never rest till she got more & more & dear Papa wld find himself in terrible trouble & difficulty.

I do *most earnestly* ask him to *pause* & put it off at least for a time – & to think, that the difficulty of doing so – or even of breaking off such an engagement is *infinitely less* than the *pain* & *suffering* of hurting all those he loves best & of offending his best friends & subjects by such a marriage which would be the inevitable result. Let him remember how dear Mama disapproved of Uncle Henry's[1] marriage & what her feelings wld be sld. she have thought of his doing the same.

For all our sakes I entreat him to delay *at any* rate so serious & I must fear, fatal a step.

Ever your devoted & loving Grandmama<br>V.R.I.

The Queen's practice of letter-writing to her grandchild was not broken by their living together in the same palace in Darmstadt. Having said what she thought, and no doubt forcefully, she committed it to paper for confirmation, and – luckily for us – posterity.

Alas for the Queen, and all the Hessian family and court, not only did the Grand Duke Ludwig IV disregard the Queen's appeal not to marry this divorced Russian commoner; he actually married her secretly, in the Neues Palais, immediately after his daughter's wedding. When they began to recover from the shock, it became the Prince of Wales's task to inform the Grand Duke that there would have to be an immediate annulment. The British ambassador in Berlin, Lord Ampthill, was ordered by the Queen to persuade the German government to speed the annulment, and the marriage was dissolved on 9 July 1884.

It was a miserable time for everyone, not least for the Grand Duke, who was shocked at the consequences of displeasing the Queen and breaking protocol. The event also took the edge off Louis's and Victoria's happiness at the start of their honeymoon, which began at Heiligenberg.

One love secret of the Queen's eventful visit to Darmstadt still remained intact on her return to England for fear of upsetting her further. The younger Battenberg boy, Prince Henry ('Liko'), had fallen in love with Princess Beatrice, and his love had been returned with ardour. It was the Queen's firm intention that her youngest daughter should remain indefinitely as her companion. It was for this reason that handsome and suitable men – including Prince Louis himself – had as far as possible been kept clear of

[1] Henry, Prince of Hesse (1838–1900), married a commoner.

this nice, dumpy, shy young Princess. But in the full throes of the emotional turmoil at Darmstadt, the two had contrived to meet often and to speak of love. When Liko saw Beatrice off at the railway station, it was agreed that a suitable time some weeks ahead would be chosen by Beatrice herself to break the news to her mother.

We shall read shortly what effect the news had on the Queen when it could no longer be kept from her.

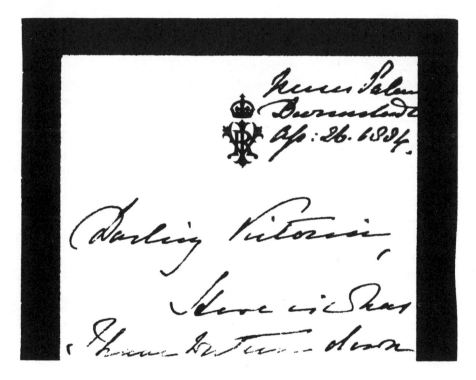

NEUES PALAIS, DARMSTADT

Ap 26 1884

Darling Victoria,

Here is what I have written down in repetition of what I said to you on Wednesday on that most distressing subject. You can show it [to] dear Papa when you like. Aunt Vicky I know shares my opinion.

Darling child, how I feel for you all in this gt. trouble wh. has come at a moment when your dear mind & heart shld. be free from sorrow & trouble. Let me once more say how I hope you will always remember *that* the *Husband must* be the person to *look up to* & *obey* – & that a woman can only really be happy & in her right place when she *can* do so. I am sure you will find this in dear Louis & what he asks you to do – you may be sure will be right.

At the same time a good & sensible wife shld. always tell her Husband what *she* thinks right or wrong & try & be a *real helpmate* to him.

This is *my* little lecture which as a loving *Mother* (for I feel I *am that* to you beloved Children *far more* than a Grandmother) I am sure you will not think a *bore* like poor Bender's[1] wld. be. Let me further ask you that when *you* are in England or here, – you will *always* turn to *me* for advice about your health or anything in which you are both in doubt. Tell this & show this *after* your marriage to dear Louis. You can also show him the enclosed when dear Papa has seen it.

God bless & preserve you darling Child! It is a terrible grief that beloved Uncle Leopold is not here – as He so much wished to be – but I am sure *you* will think of Him & His dear Spirit will be near you on that day.

Ever your devoted Grandmama & *Mother*

V.R.I.

I do not mention here today – *how* we must all feel most terribly the want of your precious Mama – but ask for *Her* blessing & she will give it.

There were few joys and many sadnesses for the Queen in 1884. One of the few happy occasions, the wedding of her favourite grand-daughter, had been darkened by the unacceptable marriage of her father. To console him, the Queen invited the heartbroken Grand Duke to England. But even deer-stalking around Balmoral, usually one of his great pleasures in life, failed to lift his depression.

The blow about Beatrice still lay some weeks ahead. But the dreaded marriage of dear Ella to her Russian Grand Duke was not calculated to lift the Queen's depression or offset her grief at the loss of her son, Leopold.

The wedding at St Petersburg was immensely grand and ostentatious in the Russian (and *not* the Queen's) tradition. 'Ella bore the fatigues remarkably well, in spite of the great weight of her dress and jewels', Victoria wrote to the Queen, whose interest in the event was in no way diminished by her disapproval of it. Although Ella would now be mountainously rich, far richer than

---

[1] Pastor Bender was Chaplain to Grand Duke Ludwig IV.

Queen Victoria whose measure of wealth was despised by the
Romanoffs, Victoria assured her grandmother that Ella would
not be spoilt by all her jewelry and palaces.

WINDSOR CASTLE

May 20 1884

Darling Victoria,

   Your dear letter touched me so much. I cannot say how it pleased
me. – I am vy. sad at the thought of tomorrow's parting for poor dear
Papa is in *such* a state of distress & grief that it is terrible to see. You
will, I know do *all* you can for him, for he feels your both marrying
terribly. All this happening at the same moment when he has had this
gt. shock & distress & when all that he (vainly & so unfortunately)
fancied was to be the source of gt. happiness is terrible for him – & I
quite fear he may be ill. – He was so much better here this fortnight but
tonight he is as bad as he was at Darmstadt.

   Take care of yourself dear Child, don't ride too much & above *all not*
if you were not *regular* in other *respects*. It *might* injure your health for
ever. Don't mind my saying this – but you know I am so anxious for
your happiness & health & strength & no one else may tell you,

Ever your devoted Grandmama

V.R.I.

BALMORAL CASTLE

June 13 1884

Darling Victoria,

   I am longing to hear from you. It is so long since we heard & we are
so far off.

   Ella must not write anything *confidential* except by the English messenger. That I know from Marie. Of course ordinary things is [*sic*]
different.

   I send something I got today for Ludwig to see. I wish we cld. get
the letters back or see them burnt.[1] It is not safe to leave them with her.

   We are very quiet here & very sad. Poor Aunty misses dear Uncle
most dreadfully & more & more at every step.

Your loving Grandmama

V.R.I.

   [1] This would appear to be a reference to letters from the Grand Duke of
Hesse retained by Madame de Kolemine.

Darling Victoria, June 27 1884

I hope to hear your Voyage has been a good one.

So *many* loving thanks for your one dear letter from St Petersburg. Everything seems to have gone off uncommonly well & been most splendid – but I hope that Darling Ella won't be spoilt by all this admiration & adulation & all this glitter of jewelry & grandeur etc.?

Lady Thornton wrote to me everyone was so pleased with her.

I send for Ludwig the copy of a letter from Aunt Vicky & one from Ld. Ampthill (wh please return) on the same subject. It is very hopeless I fear – & at any rate I think Sandro & Vicky & At. Vicky shld. let matters rest for the present & Sandro do everything he can to secure his position. But Bismarck behaves very ill.

Poor dear Papa is being shamefully teazed by everybody to marry at once – wh. makes me furious – & I have told Wernher & others abt. it. Dear Papa writes very indignantly abt. it.

We have such awful heat that I can hardly write & feel dreadfully oppressed & exhausted by it so I must end in a hurry – hoping soon to hear from Ludwig. Aunty sends many loves.

Ever your devoted Grandmama

V.R.I.

I hope you are well & Ludwig quite recovered.

Darling Victoria, Sept 29 1884

I have not yet thanked you for your dear last letter; let me do so now & say also that I think it was far wiser & better that you did not come up here, much as I regretted not seeing you – as you wld have seen but little of dear Papa – & probably got overtired at Abergeldie by the irregular hours, etc. Dear Papa is upon the whole in better spirits, seems to be comfortable and happy here – Irène is in such good looks & very dear & nice & trying to do what she can for dear Papa.

I hope you walk regularly every day? It is the one thing to be attended to.[1]

I am glad to hear Liko is going on well – but how annoying that this shld. happen.

I *have* spoken to Uncle Bertie & also shown him some of the letters & he has expressed himself very kindly. I enclose a copy of his letter to me this mng. wh. I thought Ludwig wld. like to see. Hoping soon to hear from you both.

Ever your devoted Grandmama

V.R.I.

[1] Victoria, now Princess Louis of Battenberg, was with child.

The dear little children are all quite well, & little 'Charlie'[1] quite a pretty healthy looking baby – very like dear Uncle Leopd. – his eyes quite remarkably so – Uncle Bertie jumps rather quickly to a conclusion for we have not got so far yet.

BALMORAL CASTLE

Oct 11 1884

Darling Victoria,

For 3 or 4 days I have been intending to write to you to thank you for your dear letter & to say that I think it is necessary for you now to look out for a *nurse* (*not* the monthly one) – & I have heard of 2 with the very best recommendations. The one is 38 – has gt. experience – & the other is 25 – also excellent. The 1st cld. come for £35 to £40 – & the 2nd for £35 to £36. No good Nurse wld. come for less – *now*.[2] The 1st is recommended by Chapman the excellent Nurse of Uncle Arthur's children, & the other by Creak who is with dear Uncle Leopd's children, under whom she was nursery maid. She gives her the very highest character. But 25 is rather young.

I fear you cld. not & wld not perhaps like to see them yourself. But cld. Mary Adams see one of them in London & tell you what *she* thought of them, & I wld. meantime get all the recommendations wh. were wished.

Dear Papa is well – & we are so happy to have him with us – as we love him so much – but he is often very sad & very depressed & I fear all these appeals of that dreadful woman[3] worry & distress him *terribly*.

If only an end cld. be put to it & if this dreadful woman cld. be seen by *him* in the *true light* & he never see her or hear from her! But she has written to him again only just now – wanting to have the whole urtheil veröffentlicht.[4] He sent the letter to Lothersen & did not answer it. He is so worried & distressed that he *ought* to, & *must get away*. Uncle Bertie is very strong abt. it, so are some of his people & all of us. He will never be able to break with the *whole* thing & with her – unless he gets quite away – & the opportunity to visit Uncle Arthur who leaves

[1] Charles Edward, Son of Prince Leopold, later Duke of Saxe-Coburg-Gotha (1884–1954).

[2] Inflation, it seems, is no new thing. These are, of course, per annum wages.

[3] Mme Alexandrine de Kolemine, though paid off handsomely with a life pension and the title Countess of Romrod, and later re-marrying, continued to be a pest, and there are suggestions of blackmail in her behaviour. See letter of 13 June.

[4] Verdict published.

in April – may never present itself again. His remaining at Darmstadt or in the neighbourhood wld. keep up the whole thing & annoy him dreadfully. *Believe* me it is *the only* thing to cheer him up & set him again. He shld. go to India after Christmas & be back the middle or end of March.

I assure you it is the *only* thing for him to do.

I must end my letter. I am grieved to hear that you have had to have S [illegible] again. I direct this to the Royal Yacht[1] but wonder if you are living there.

Ever your devoted Grandmama<br>V.R.I.

The news of Princess Beatrice's love for the Battenberg Prince, Liko, and his intention of marrying her if the Queen would give her consent, had at last been broken to her by her daughter. The effect was all that Beatrice had feared, and at first the Queen would not allow her to speak further of the possibility. The young couple slowly wore down the Queen's resistance, and the engagement was formally announced on 30 December 1884. The price of agreement was high, however. Princess Beatrice was to continue with her duties as a sort of personal assistant to the Queen, and Prince Henry must make his home in England – which really meant living with his mother-in-law for the rest of his life.

BALMORAL CASTLE

Nov 14 1884

Darling Victoria,

Your dear letter of the 11th recd. yesterday gave me & Auntie (to whom I showed it) great pleasure. As I wrote to Ludwig I am becoming more reconciled to the possibility of this event. Of course it remains a shock to me, & there will be things very difficult to get over with my feelings – Still as he is so amiable & prepared to do what I wish – I hope all may be for the best & may turn out well. Of course I *can't* spare Auntie, & especially at first they must *not* think of travelling or paying visits.

I suppose Liko will not be able to get longer leave than the 2nd or 3rd Jany. or can he stay longer?

I was sure you wld be dreadfully shocked at poor Capt. Thomson's[2]

[1] Louis had been appointed to the Royal Yacht *Victoria and Albert,* and the couple had rented a house near Portsmouth.

[2] Captain Frank Thomson, R.N., Captain of the Royal Yacht *Victoria and Albert.*

death. – I have sent thro Auntie the acct. of his short & dreadful illness, to Ludwig.

I am so delighted to hear you are so well unberufen & so prudent. How is Frau Strecken[1] & all my acquaintances. I am much interested in the Duke of Brunswick's Will for I hear that it is most likely that a large part of the personal property in money is to be divided between his nearest of Kin wh. includes your Father-in-law! What have you & Papa heard about it?

Only think poor old Willie Blair, the old Fiddler who always played at our Gay Balls *here*, & who had done so ever since we came to the country in 48 – & long before – died on Tuesday aged *90*!

*Every*, every *link* with the *past* is being swept away!

I hope Liko will practise his Music – as you know what an essential thing that is for Auntie, & English also.

With love *to all*,

Ever your devoted Grandmama

V.R.I.

We leave this on the *19th*. Since yesterday, we have very frosty but beautifully bright weather.

WINDSOR CASTLE

Dec 8 1884

Darling Victoria.

Instead of answering Ludwig & thanking him for his interesting & *satisfactory* letter recd. today – I write to *you*, because there is *something* in his letter wh. I must just *ask you* about.

I understand that the *last time* you were *unwell* – ended on the 17th May? & that you felt sick already when you returned from Russia at the end of June. This led me to calculate[2] that the event shld. take place between the 20th & 27th or so of Feb: & this was what Dr Hoffmeister thought. Now Ludwig writes you only felt the 1st movement at the end of Oct: wh. you thought was at 4 months & ½. Now are you sure of that? It is often so slight at 1st that one hardly knows. It differs so much with different people that one can hardly *rely on that* for time. Still I must ask you to tell me as well *as you can* abt. the *1st dates*, as I am anxious to make *all as safe* as *possible* abt. the Doctor & Nurse.

I am so thankful to hear you are so well & trust the journey will not

[1] Vice-President of the Princess Alice Hospital and manager of the Darmstadt charities.

[2] There was no surer gynaecological adviser than the Queen, who had borne nine children, and was deeply interested in every aspect of every pregnancy in her family.

tire you too much. I think we shall go to Osborne on the 17th – You will I hope stay with us in the House till the 22nd.

The Christening[1] at Claremont was *very touching*. I enclose for *you all* to read – an account of it written by Ldy. Abercromby.[2] Poor dear Aunt Helen[3] was gtly tried but behaved so courageously tho' she was nearly breaking down often, but she bore up till it was all over. Little Charlie is quite a fine, big boy, & very like dear Uncle Leopold.

I will write to dear Papa on Wednesday.

Ever your devoted Grandmama
V.R.I.

Pray answer me *as soon* as you can & *before you leave*.


Victoria gave birth to her first child, a girl, on 24 February 1885, in the same room in Windsor Castle in which she had been born, the Queen acting as extra accoucheuse on both occasions. She was named Victoria Alice Elizabeth Julie Marie. Princess Alice, eldest sister of Earl Mountbatten of Burma, married Prince Andrew of Greece in 1903. Her last child is the present Duke of Edinburgh.


IN THE TRAIN BETWEEN DIJON AND CHALON
Ap 1 1885

Darling Victoria,

Forgive this very bad writing but the train shakes dreadfully. I was so sorry to take leave of you both, for you *both* are like my Children & I hope you will often come to us, for you will have a double reason for doing so on acct. of Liko. After having seen you almost every day for more than 3 months, & every day for 6 weeks & living in the same House – we shall miss you very much. I hope you & Baby & poor Mary Adams did not suffer from the very cold night & early move in the cold? – Since 12, it is very hot as the sun is very strong. Dijon seems to have a fine Cathedral & *before* coming to it the country is rocky & hilly, but since, up to now, it is very flat. You see nothing but vineyards – immense tracts of them.

Do give dear Papa (to whom I will write tomorrow) & 'the others' many loves & my affte. regards to your Parents-in-Law & love to Marie E. [Erbach] & of course to dear Liko who I was sorry not to see this

---

[1] The late 'Uncle Leopold's' son, Charles Edward. (See footnote 1, page 68.)

[2] Lady of the Bedchamber to Queen Victoria 1874–85.

[3] The Duke of Albany's widow.

mng but I was asleep. We have just come to Chalon (not Châlon*s*). I see it is a gt. junction & called Chalon St Côme et sur Saone.

I must ask you to let me have a copy of your admirable letter to Uncle Bertie. I shld wish to keep it.

– Maison Mottet, Aix les Bains.

We arrived here at 20 m.p. 6[1] quite safely – but I am a good deal tired as it was very hot & the train shook very much. The scenery here is quite splendid – like Switzerland & the Lago Maggiore & some of our large Scotch Lochs, & indeed the whole way after Ambérieu – thro the Jura Mountains up to here is very fine & grand. The House is very nice & comfortable – but at 1*st* I always feel (& *now* after such sad changes since I went to a *new* place – specially) rather low & forlorn in a new House.

We are thinking & talking so much of you! – I am always longing to know what you & Baby are doing. Good Mrs Brotherstone[2] is better but not able to be up yet.

It is most tiresome. But it is only a bilious attack.

I hear poor Daisy[3] was much distressed at our leaving, poor little darling.

God bless you

Ever your devoted Grandmama<br>V.R.I.

It is very provoking that you shld. have to return alone to Darmstadt without Louis & you will I fear feel the separation much. He is so good & kind & *so* devoted to you. You must be very good & *not* stand abt. yet. But walk a little in the garden. It is not cold here.


MAISON MOTTET, AIX LES BAINS

3rd Ap 1885

Darling Victoria,

*Many, many* happy returns of your dear birthday wh. I grieve to think you will spend without dear Ludwig – who loves you *so* dearly, the 1st time after your marriage. He will feel it very much for he will be *quite alone* – & I pity him! My gifts are: a Locket for Baby's hair & an enamel of Ella wh. tho' not quite new, wld. I thought remind you of the time when you were together in Scotland & England with us! – The accts.

---

[1] Twenty minutes past six.

[2] A nurse. She was in attendance at the birth of Princess Alice, later Countess of Athlone.

[3] Princess Margaret of Connaught, born 1882.

of the Affghan difficulty[1] are very unsatisfactory & Russia is behaving *very ill*. I can't help hoping that something or other may *oblige* Serge to go back *before* I come leaving Ella there for the Confirmation. Affairs are so very threatening that it wld be *very awkward* for me to meet a Grand-duke then. I hope however War may still be averted.

We have marvellously fine weather & the country is splendid. We have taken 2 such beautiful drives, – today especially – & the Mountains are so close & so wild & grand. The Lac Bourget is lovely – & the colour of it – like that of Lago Maggiore & even of the Mediterranean.

This afternoon in our drive we saw the snowy range of the Alps – rising above the other high mountains, wh. was a pleasure to me as I so delight in mountains & hills. You surely know those beautiful lines of Byron's Poem of 'The Island'?

> 'He who first met the Highland's swelling blue
> 'Will love each peak wh. shows a kindred hue
> 'Hail in each crag a friend's familiar face
> 'And clasp the Mountain in his mind's embrace'

I always *feel that* in mountainous countries.

I hope *you* will speak to dear Papa abt. the 'hoheit'[2] & also abt. the 'Royal Highness'.[3]

I must now conclude. Let me just add what I said before, *how* I have learnt to esteem your dear Louis – what a motherly feeling I have for him & what an exceptionally tender kind & excellent Husband you have in him! – You can *never* show him too much devotion & affection.

And now good bye & God bless you.

Love to dear Papa & *all*.

What does Papa say to his Gd Child & what does Orchie think of her?

Ever your devoted Grandmama

V.R.I.

I hope Mary A.[4] is well & Mary Jones[5] gets on well?

[1] The occupation of Merv by Russia had intensified the dispute between Russia and Britain, who believed that the security of India was in jeopardy. An Anglo-Russian commission was appointed and a protocol was signed at St Petersburg 22 July 1887.

[2] Highness.

[3] The Queen had conferred the title of 'Royal Highness' on Prince Henry of Battenberg, previously a German 'Serene Highness', on his marriage to Princess Beatrice. This had angered Willy her grandson, the future Emperor of Germany—one more round in the eternal fight between Prussia and Hesse. The Queen's request suggests that the Grand Duke is to try to take the heat out of the situation.

[4] Mary Adams, the nurse referred to in the letter of 11 October 1884.

[5] The nurse who attended Victoria at the birth of her daughter.

WINDSOR CASTLE

May 14 1885

Darling Victoria,

Tho' I shall see you on Saturday wh. will be a great pleasure, I wish to write a little line to thank you for your dear letter, tho I am very tired from my 3 days (not quite 3) in London.

I am glad the Country is looking so pretty, so it is here – but so far more backward than in Germany & Savoy, No horse chestnut blossom out hardly yet. I have heard from dear Papa & from Irène.

I am very pleased that you liked the book I gave you & there are 2 or 3 others by this American wh. I think wld. equally interest you. While I am the *1st* to abhor hypocrisy I think that you go too far in that view & that you don't quite think enough, darling Child, of the comfort & blessing there is, in *feeling* that there *is* an all powerful & loving Father who watches over us & overrules all for the best & that we have another & better World to look forward to, where we shall *not* be parted. This, & the other books I have spoken [of] *show* clearly *how* we cannot understand *how all* will be, but how clearly we can understand & trust that there *is* that Eternal Home.

You must not, darling Child, be vexed at my saying this but I love you too dearly not to feel anxious that you shld. think seriously of *these* things without wh. Life becomes so unreal – & one *can* have no comfort or support in times of trial & sorrow.

The Guards are to return & I was able to announce this to poor Amy[1] who has been so good & brave before we left London. Auntie's 'Dot'[2] was proposed today & I hear was only opposed by Labouchère & some Irishmen but not in violent language & the introduction was carried by a majority of 337 to 38!

On Saturday we are going from here to Netley & expect to be back about 7. Uncle Alfred & Auntie Marie are also coming here on that day.

I am longing to see how much Baby has grown in this fortnight.

Love to Ludwig who Liko will be so glad to see, & believe me always,

Your devoted Grandmama
V.R.I.

Queen Victoria dreaded the emotional strain she would suffer at the wedding of her youngest child, and she insisted that the ceremony should be performed in the little village church at

[1] See footnote 1 page 54.

[2] Princess Beatrice's dowry on her marriage, the subject of adverse comment in Parliament from some anti-royalist members.

Whippingham in the Isle of Wight, rather than in London, in order to reduce the crowds. The Queen cried a little but otherwise gave no evidence of the grief she had earlier claimed she would experience. *Truth* magazine, commenting on the speed of Liko's responses, wrote waspishly: 'It is not vouchsafed to all of us to become demorganaticated, bridegrooms, Royal Highnesses, and Knights of the Garter in the twinkling of an eye.' The marriage took place on 23 July 1885.

WINDSOR CASTLE

July 11 1885

Darling Victoria,

Tho' we shall meet tomorrow – I write a line to thank you for your last dear letter – & ask you to come over in the Alberta[1] to meet us. I am dreading the heat but long for a little rest – for me but as much for you. Auntie who was quite overdone by most touching kindness, had really *too much* to do – packing, dividing & things [*sic*] writing letters of thanks etc. – And I am *very depressed*. How I dread the week after next – & how I wish it was months and years off! The nearer the fatal day approaches the more my invincible dislike to Auntie's marriage (*not* to dear Liko) – increases. Sometimes I feel as if *I never* cld. take her myself to the Marriage Service – & that I wld. wish to run away & hide myself!

The departure & that evn^g will be awful for me. I fear I shall be a very stupid Host & not be able to *entertain* your Parents-in-Law as I shld wish. But my heart will be *so* sore – & then the absence of those who wld. have taken such interest, & the recollection of the last English Wedding is so very full of pain & Wehmuth,[2] that it will be very trying. It is not 3 months over 3 years that poor dear Uncle Leopold was married & not 2 years after that tie was broken!

I long to see little Alice who must be brought up to the Wedding breakfast.

Ever your devoted Grandmama

V.R.I.

You must help us & Uncle Arthur is most kind & helpful

Queen Victoria did not believe her grand-daughter's character was unreformable just because she was now married and a mother. Victoria's brisk and impatient ways and her enquiring

[1] A small yacht attached to the Royal Yacht *Victoria and Albert*.
[2] Melancholy.

mind still gave the Queen concern, more so because she loved her dearly. But the Queen was quite wrong in her judgement of Victoria's relations with her husband. '. . . these strictures . . . failed to take into account that Louis, who had known Victoria from infancy, saw what he was in for and recognized his own need for an exacting marriage. . . . He loved her restless mind, just as Prince Albert had enjoyed the Queen's intelligence and analytical skills.'[1]

OSBORNE

Aug 21 1885

Darling Victoria,

I cld. not say much – but the sight of you all going away & the feeling that the dear little Establishment at Kent House[2] was broken up – made me *very* sad! – May you sometimes return to spend a Spring or summer or winter there. For Liko's sake I wish it much – & should *another* Event[3] ever take place – England wld be better than Germany.

Let me again ask you to remember that your *1st duty* is to your dear & most devoted *Husband* to whom you can *never* be *kind enough* & to whom I think a *little* more tenderness is due *sometimes*.

He is so good a son that I am sure his great wish will be to aid you in every way to be a comfort & support to poor dear Papa. You must watch over him & be *very particular yourself* as to *who* you see & make more intimate acquaintance with & in *this* dear Ludwig will surely help you – your Parents-in-Law too can give you *good advice*. Pray be also very attentive & loving to them, for they have now *no* Child at home!

I asked Ludwig to give you a letter for Prss. Battenberg from me.

Lastly let me add one word wh. as your *Godmother* as well as Grandmama I may. It is *not* to neglect going to Church or to *read* some good & serious religious book, *not materialistic* & *controversial* ones – for they are very bad for *everyone* – but *especially* for *young* people.

And now darling Victoria, I will end my long *lecture* with a kiss to you & *Baby* & many loves to dear Papa & sisters

Ever your devoted loving Grandmama

V.R.I.

[1] *Louis and Victoria: the first Mountbattens* (1974) by Richard Hough.

[2] Near Osborne in the Isle of Wight. It later became the property of Princess Louise, Duchess of Argyll, and was made over to Victoria shortly before the First World War.

[3] The Queen means a second baby. But another four years were to pass before Victoria gave birth to her next child, Princess Louise, later Queen of Sweden.

'I write to thank you for your last dear letter & to send you these Photos of me in *my* Jubilee Dress.' Queen Victoria to Princess Victoria 26 August 1887.

Princess Victoria with her father, the Grand Duke of Hesse, and her first child,
Princess Alice. Prince Louis stands behind. The year is 1885.

Princess Victoria on the day of her wedding, 30 April 1884. 'I think that you have done well to choose only a Husband who is *quite* of your way of thinking & who in many respects is as English as you are,' commented the Queen on Prince Louis of Battenberg.

Queen Victoria and Princess Victoria depart from Osborne for a carriage drive, Summer 1890.

Windsor Castle: a contemporary photograph.

Osborne House, Isle of Wight.

The New Palace and the old schloss, Darmstadt, 1897. The signatures are those of the Empress of Russia, Princess Alexandra; Victoria Melita, the Grand Duchess; Ernst-Ludwig, the Grand Duke; Alfred ('Affie'), Duke of Saxe-Coburg-Gotha; Nicholas, Emperor of All the Russias; and the place card of Miss Nona Kerr, Lady-in-Waiting to Princess Victoria, for whom these signatures were made.

ILLINSKOE · 1901

Grand Duchess Ella's country estate outside Moscow. The occasion is a visit by Princess Victoria and her husband, Prince Louis of Battenberg. *Top, left to right,* Princess Victoria playing with the children; Prince George of Battenberg, now nine years old; Prince Louis. *Lower, left to right* The family at tea shows Grand Duke Serge studying a book. He was assassinated four years later. The present Lord Mountbatten's first pony ride. His older sister Princess Louise at Wolfsgarten.

The Hessian daughters as young women. *Left to right*, Princesses Alix (future Tsarina), Victoria, Elizabeth ('Ella') and Irène.

Nicky's and Alix's engagement photograph, 1894. They were Tsar and Tsarina by the end of the year.

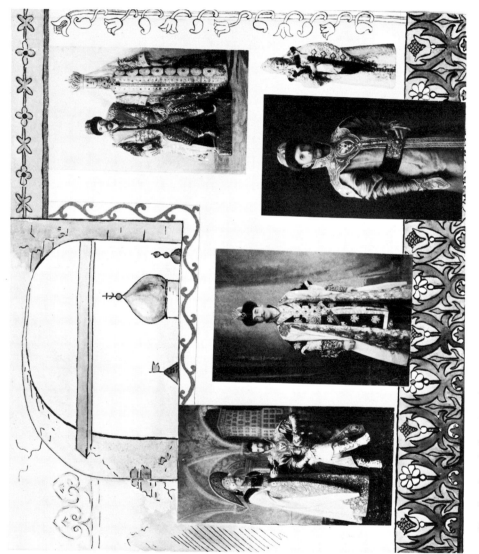

Russian theatricals at Tsarkoe-Selo, starring the Emperor and Empress (*top right*) and the Grand Duke and Grand Duchess Serge. Decorations by Princess Victoria's sisters, Alicky and Ella.

Hessian-Battenberg gathering at Heiligenberg. Victoria on the right wearing the boater has Princess Alice (Prince Philip's mother) on her lap; her father the Grand Duke is above her; her husband extreme right. In the centre of the group is Prince Louis's mother, Princess Julie of Battenberg, and in the foreground Victoria's young brother, Ernst-Ludwig, the future Grand Duke of Hesse.

Princess Victoria with her first child, Princess Alice.

Princess Victoria in 1894, now married for ten years, with her three children, Alice (future Princess Andrew of Greece), Louise (future Queen of Sweden) and little Georgie.

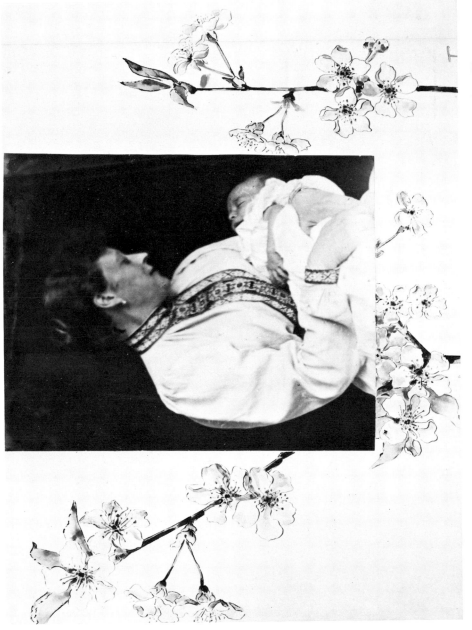

Princess Victoria with the infant Louis ('Dickie' Mountbatten), 1900. Decorations by Miss Nona Kerr.

Family 'snaps' at Heiligenberg. Grand Duke 'Ernie' provided the pre-surrealist decorations.

Princess Victoria's parents, Princess Alice and Grand Duke Ludwig IV of Hesse.

'Vicky' and 'Fritz', Princess
Victoria's aunt, and uncle by
marriage, Crown Prince and
Princess and future German
Emperor and Empress.

'Affie' and 'Marie', Princess Victoria's uncle, and aunt by marriage, Duke and Duchess of Edinburgh and future Duke and Duchess of Saxe-Coburg-Gotha.

Louise, Marchioness of Lorne, and John, Marquess of Lorne, Princess Victoria's aunt, and uncle by marriage, and future Duke and Duchess of Argyll.

The Prince of Wales, Princess Victoria's uncle.

Prince Leopold, Duke of Albany, Princess Victoria's uncle.

Princess Beatrice, Princess Victoria's aunt and the Queen's last child. She was
only six years older than her niece.

A brave and tragic figure, Princess Victoria's brother-in-law Prince Alexander of Battenberg, 'Sandro'.

Meanwhile, as the next letter (1 September) reveals, the Queen rapidly developed a close affection for her new son-in-law, Liko. As the years passed she increasingly came to depend on him for the sound advice and steady guidance he gave her, in the tradition of Prince Albert.

BALMORAL CASTLE

Sept 1 1885

Darling Victoria,

I must write you a line to thank you for your dear letter from Buckingham Palace in wh. you promised to remember my little Winke.[1]

I thought you wld like to hear how well all is going on – how nice & sensible dear Liko is, how happy dear Auntie is & they are together – & yet so sensibly etc. – so that I feel but little change. Liko is delighted to go out stalking but not to go out 2 days running away from Auntie.

We have not had a drop of rain since we came, but till Sunday we had hardly any sun, & it was cold. The grass & trees were however so beautifully green that it was quite refreshing after poor burnt up Osborne with the leaves turning & dropping off & the grass quite brown. Here we have the Lime Trees just blooming, quantities of wild roses – beautiful roses in the garden, delicious strawberries & peas!! And the heather quite wonderfully brilliant. Since Sunday we have beautiful bright days – & hot sun but alas! 2 frosts of 7 deg: wh have spoilt all the poor people's potatoes – & I fear the flowers have suffered & I dread the leaves of the trees! Such sharp frosts – so early – are quite unusual. I trust it won't continue.

You will of course have heard from Ludwig what a very unfortunate & bad voyage his last in the Yacht was & how the pleasure trip has ended?

How fortunate you did not go!

I was so sorry to wish Louis goodbye & he seemed to feel it very much.

I must end in great haste. Irène will have told you abt the reception here.

Ever your devoted Mama [*sic*]

V.R.I.

[1] Hints.

BALMORAL CASTLE

Sept 29 1885

Darling Victoria,

*What* a terrible anxiety[1] this has been & is & *how* I have felt for you all & dear Sandro *I cannot* tell you.

Unfortunate it is – just at this moment, but I have gt. hopes that *all* will come right. I have written & telegraphed very strongly & I think with success.

The Gov*t.* is *most* anxious to *keep* Sandro where he is – & Sir Wm. White is to take part in the Conference at Constantinople & to support Sandro *if* he will try & prevent Macedonia from rising & *not* disarm hastily the Muselmans. We have telegraphed to him in this sense.

Poor dear Liko is very anxious but very sensible. But it is a terrible worry. – Mr Smith[2] (the War Minister) who is here is very wise & sensible & full of sympathy for poor dear Sandro.

Uncle A. & Aunt L.[3] have told us a good deal abt. Wolfsgarten etc. & abt. your 2 *Cousins* & the odd manner etc. of V.H.[4] Pray *sit upon* her a little & don't let her be forward & *try* to dictate. You shld. *all* do that. They ought not to have come without a Governess for so long.

We have had some very cold weather but it was a snow storm only lasting 3 days – & yesterday & today are lovely.

How is dear little Baby? *Is* she photographed?

Thank Ludwig very much for his letter, say the *Pictures* or Sketches have not arrived.

We shall miss Ernie dreadfully. He is such a dear, dear Boy & such a favourite. He must *not* be treated like a little Boy[5] – for he is extremely sensible & cld be a gt. help to Papa.

Love to all

From your devoted Grandmama

V.R.I.

Many thanks for your last dear letter.

[1] The southern Bulgars, nominally under the rule of Turkey, had rebelled and thrust themselves under the more liberal rule of northern Bulgaria, governed by Sandro. Serbia invaded the country and was routed by Sandro at the battle of Slivnitza. But later, under strong Russian pressure, Sandro was forced to abdicate. The Queen, who always claimed pacifist principles, adored heroism on the field of battle, especially in her relations.

[2] William Henry Smith (1825–91), newsagent, bookseller and statesman.

[3] Prince Arthur, Duke of Connaught, and his wife Louise.

[4] Princess Helena Victoria, elder daughter of Princess Helena and Prince Christian of Schleswig-Holstein.

[5] Prince Ernst-Ludwig was now 16¾.

WINDSOR CASTLE

Dec 9 1885

Darling Victoria,

I have not yet written to thank you for the charming Photographs of dear little Baby Alice who must be so pretty, & for your last dear letter of the 17 Nov. accompanying them. I am so glad she is quite well now[1] – only I hope she will soon begin to have some teeth.

We are constantly occupied with Bulgaria & dear Sandro's wonderful success & splendid conduct. *No one cld* sympathise *more truly* with your anxiety & your joy & pride, than I do. How proud you must all be of him! Please God! all looks so much better now.

Our Elections wh. began so well have not gone on so – but still the Moderate Liberals have conquered the extreme Radicals in England, & everywhere the Minorities have been so much larger. – In Ireland *not* one Liberal has come in, but a few Conservatives & nearly 70 Nationalists or Parnellites! – This will be a gt. difficulty. Dear Auntie has been very poorly with the effects of a bad chill but she is nearly quite well again & Liko is very well. But poor Aunt Lenchen is entirely confined to her bed – also from the effects of a bad chill she got I think at Homburg or Darmstadt.

Do tell Ludwig that Millar's 2 Pictures of [illegible] for Christmas are extremely pretty. At. Vicky was much pleased with the Picture he painted for her birthday.

We are *furious* & *indignant* beyond words at what has been done by the Gotha Almanack[2] wh. *ought* to be protested against. It is perfectly monstrous! And they have done the same to the Tecks! –

We have very sharp frost since 2 days, & I think it will freeze again. We go on the 17th or 18th to Osborne & I shall think so much of you & miss you both, much.

Ever your devoted Grandmama

V.R.I.

[1] A little later the infant Princess Alice was found to be almost stone deaf, a disability she overcame with remarkable courage. She learned to lip-read in three languages by the time she was fifteen.

[2] After thirty-three years, and without notice, the Almanack (the pre-eminent guide to Royal and aristocratic status and genealogy) had de-rated the Battenbergs and Tecks from Part I (the super élite) to Part II where they now rubbed shoulders with lesser Dukes like Atholl and Beaufort, and even Counts like the loathed Bismarck. The Queen was outraged and regarded this act as a personal insult to herself as well as her loved relations. She suspected the German Empress was behind the plot.

Queen Victoria's suspicion of Russia – 'that horrid, corrupt country' – endured for all her life. This continued to lead to serious strains and hints of rifts with her Hessian relatives, whom she loved as her own, but themselves had so many close ties with the Romanoffs.

Sometimes one feels that the poor widowed Grand Duke Ludwig IV could never do a thing right in his mother-in-law's eyes. He never did re-marry.

WINDSOR CASTLE

Feb 20 1886

Darling Victoria,

I *do* believe it is nearly 2 months since you wrote to me & that *you* have not *written to me* once in *this* year!!! You naughty child, I have also not written but I miss your letters very much. I had a kind one from Ludwig just a month ago from London.

I must tell you *how* annoyed & *grieved* I am at dear Papa & Irène's going to Petersburg – *now* – so soon after the monstrous way in wh dear Sandro has been treated & in fact *is* so still! I think it *most* unfortunate. And then for poor Irène, it is most awkward for no end of reports have been spread, & I *know* that Olga Cécile[1] is *bent* upon Micha's marrying her! I shall *never* forgive it, if she also is to go to that horrid, corrupt Country – & I shld. break with Papa if he did it!

I feel *so strongly* about it that you must not be surprised if I express myself as I do.

Papa hinted at *his* seeing Hélène of Mecklenburg[2] with an object? *I* told him that if he *really* liked her, if she wld be kind to all of you & *keep up* dear Mama's *Memory* I cld: say nothing agnst it, but that of course the intercourse & feeling between us cld never be the same, *naturally*. I hear that she is 'plus Russe que les Russes'.

I am thinking with pleasure that you will be coming over before long & that we shall have you with us. But I wish you wld bring Baby! I have sent a little present for her 1st birthday & am making a little Hood for her. How well I remember that *dreadful* day last year!

[1] Wife of the Grand Duke Michael Nicholaievitch. She was Princess Cécile of Baden, and Micha their second son, had hoped to marry Victoria. He married Sophie, Countess of Merenberg, created Countess de Torby. Their elder daughter is Lady Zia Wernher, widow of Sir Harold Wernher. The younger daughter, Nada, married Victoria's elder son, George.

[2] Princess Hélène of Mecklenburg-Strelitz.

Dear little Alice Albany who is quite a charming child is here with her Mama & brother & will spend her birthday here.

I used your charming blotting book *constantly* at Osborne where it will remain & it is most useful & so beautifully done. I read with gt. interest & pleasure Marie Erbach's[1] charming Reise Beschreibung (or rather Marie Leiningen read it out to me) & it is so beautifully printed. How I wish we could have someone here who cld. *print* quite privately as you did, as I often have my private things which I shld. like to get printed.

I must end hoping to hear from you very soon again.

Ever your devoted Mama [sic]<br>V.R.I.

Love to Ludwig.

WINDSOR CASTLE

July 14 1886

Darling Victoria,

Many loving thanks for your dear letter. We miss you and the darling Baby very much! I so often think of you & how interested you wld have been if you cld have seen the reception[2] of wh. I sent Irène the description. Yesterday 2 of the Indians sat to me – & Aunt Louise helped. Tomorrow morning we are going quite early to the Exhibition.

The Elections are going quite wonderfully – No losses these last 2 days at all & nothing but gains! Today 8 – the Conservatives will have above 300 & the Unionist Liberals 72. Nearly 130 majority agst the G.O.M.[3] who writes more [?] dreadful letters setting class against class – & behaves abominably. I really think he is cracked.

I send you today Bourke's Peerage[4] wh. I hope you will find useful.

Love to *all*

Ever your devoted Mama [sic]<br>V.R.I.

[1] Marie Erbach-Schönberg, wife of Count, later Prince, Gustav Erbach-Schönberg, and sister of Prince Louis of Battenberg. She had evidently written a charming account of her travels.

[2] For all the natives working on the Colonial and Indian Exhibition at South Kensington. It was in St George's Hall, Windsor Castle.

[3] The Grand Old Man, referring (ironically) to the hated Gladstone, Liberal Leader. The Queen's political prejudices were widely known by contrast with those of a century later.

[4] The Queen means *Burke's Peerage*, of course; perhaps a subconscious lapse as the Bourke family figured prominently in it.

                                           Sept 3 1886
Darling Victoria,

What dreadful anxiety we have been living in since that awful Sunday 22nd! & those 3 days before we knew where dear noble brave Sandro was! When we heard his dear life was safe[1] & the enthusiasm was so great for him, & that wicked, villainous, atrocious Russia failed – I felt as if I cld. have jumped for joy! Do tell this & read this to your dear Parents-in-Law that I really cld hardly have felt much more for my own son than I have done and do for dear Sandro. Next to *this* the interest of *all* Europe is to check Russia's monstrous claims! – And now *what* an infamous answer from the Emperor to Sandro's (*I* think *too civil*) message! It is very stupid as well as wicked of Russia for she thereby admits almost that *she approves* of the monstrous plot. I have *such* a dislike to the fat Czar. I think him a violent Paul-like Asiatic full of hate, passion & tyranny![2] And to behave like this to his *own* Cousin, so beloved of his 'Venerated Father' who would never have behaved in this way is too shocking! Many thanks for your dear letter of the 21st Aug. with accts.[3] of dear Alicky. I am rather alarmed at her being allowed out so soon. *Here never before 3 weeks* are they allowed out – as just at that time a species of dropsy shows itself – wh. is *often* very dangerous & even *fatal*. And the *slighter* the attack the *more* dangerous the *consequences*. I will send later the acct. of the procedure necessary to prevent *infection*. Till the peeling has entirely ceased & any particle of peeling still continues, the infection is not over & all woollen things or others wh. cannot wash or be scalded shld be destroyed! Considering dear Auntie's state & the dear little Children here – it wld be considered *unsafe* if Alicky came here till 6 weeks are elapsed & unless the *above* precautions *are taken*. None of us have ever had it.

We have had & are having most splendid & *very* hot weather since we came & wear our summer Clothes. The last two [day 1] the air has been cooler –

I hope my sweet little darling is well? Can she walk or speak? I will wait to write to Ludwig & thank him for his nice letter till I hear from him from Bucharest.

                              Ever your devoted Grandmama
                                           V.R.I.
Love to all.

[1] Prince Alexander, Sovereign Prince of Bulgaria, and his brother Francis Joseph ('Franzjos'), had been kidnapped by dissident Bulgarian army officers under Russian pressure, but later released.

[2] Strong words but, as usual, deserved.

[3] She probably had scarlet fever.

HOLYROOD PALACE

Darling Victoria, Oct 26 1886

It is ages since I have written to you & I write now somewhat in haste. Many thanks for your last dear letter of the 8th. I am glad you approved of the 'Hunting Stewart' sash & ribbons wh are the 1st of the sort. Daisy, Arthur & the Baby (such a beauty & so good) & little Alice Albany & Charlie have also got some.

We are immensely interested by all Franzjos tells us – & he is charming – so amiable, clever & amusing & not a bit shy. We shall be very sorry to lose him when he leaves on Saturday (30th) with dear Papa whom we shall also be so sorry to lose. We have been a very pleasant family party together & tho' a while ago we had a good deal of rain we have had charming weather again since – not cold. I never remember it so continuously mild as it has been this autumn, so many trees still green & the golden birches retaining their leaves so long. More than ever do I grieve at having for the 1st time since 16 or 17 years to leave so early as the 4th November but unfortunately Auntie cannot well remain longer & we shall have a very weary time at Windsor wh. is unpleasant & unwholesome for long at a time in the winter.

However we must make the best of it. Thank God unberufen dear Auntie[1] is so well & active & walks so well & daily. You did not walk near enough. We are happy to keep dear Irène who will have told you all we are doing. We have lately been taking long expeditions, lunching at the Danzig or lunching earlier & going out quite early as alas! the days are so short.

How pluckily & admirably the Bulgarians behave *now* & how monstrously Gnl. Kaulbars[2] behaves, clumsily too I think as the Russians show their hand too much. Do have Baby photographed as soon as possible please.

I must now end. But pray either you or Ludwig write me an acct. of your visit to Stuttgardt & what the majestären & Vera[3] said abt. Sandro's treatment. Love to Ludwig & Sandro – & a kiss to my little Baby.

Ever your devoted Grandmama

V.R.I.

[1] Beatrice, Princess Henry of Battenberg, was carrying her first child. He was born 5 November 1886 at Windsor, Prince Alexander ('Drino') of Battenberg.

[2] Russian Special Commissioner in Bulgaria. He was so hated by all classes that he provided a unifying influence and was sent home again.

[3] Charles I, King of Württemberg and his wife Olga, daughter of Tsar Nicholas I. Vera was Vera Constantinovna, Grand Duchess of Russia and widow of Duke Eugene of Württemberg.

No event sent Queen Victoria scuttling so fast to her writing
desk as a confinement in the family, more especially a dramatic
*first* one. Similar long letters to the one that follows would have
gone to countless near relations. It has never been satisfactorily
explained how she found the time, among her multitudinous
duties, to write so much. She was sixty-seven.

WINDSOR CASTLE

Nov 23 1886

Darling Victoria,

Just a few lines to tell you abt. dear Auntie who is unberufen so
wonderfully well. She was very active and took good walks daily – &
had walked down to the Mausoleum in the mng. been out with Liko
in the afternoon, took tea with us – & was just going to dress for
dinner with us – (to wh. Ld & Ly Randolph Churchill came) when the
water broke! Still we were uncertain. She cld not come to dinner of
course & Brotherstone[1] (who had *fortunately* come south on Wednesday
& was stopping with the H. Browns at the kennel) was sent for – &
when I came back from dinner Auntie was already having pains wh.
increased and became very severe & continual. The Dr (Dr Williams)
arrived at 20 m. p.12 – she went to bed at $\frac{1}{4}$ to 1 – The pains were very
severe & tedious but she was very good & brave. They feared it might
go on long – but at 4 this suddenly changed to bearing pains & at 5.10
the Baby was born! She had a gt. deal of chloroform but was very quiet
& never entirely unconscious tho' felt little pain. The whole confinement was very like my first when Aunt Vicky was born in *every* detail
Like Auntie it was *expected* in the *1st days of Dec* & happened on the *21st
Nov* – & *hers* on the *23rd* Like hers it began with the same symptoms.

The Baby is not big but very vigorous & well developed [*sic*] with a
big nose & very pretty *small ears*. I hope the eyes will be brown but I
cannot judge yet, as I have seldom seen them open. Auntie is so well &
calm – slept so well & looks so fresh & pink. She had only 9 hours to
suffer & you – 20! It is inconceivable the difference, but I think she
walked much more than you did. She is in her *own* room & the little boy
was born in the room where Uncle Alfred was born – as we had them in
*those* days. Mrs Brotherstone is very well indeed. We were delighted
with Dr Williams, he is so quiet, cheerful & encouraging. He is younger
a good deal than Dr Duncan. Dear Liko is very happy; he was very
anxious before I think, tho' he did not say so. He was very helpful &
was there continually excepting when he took a little rest while I remained. With the exception of a short time when I laid down on the

[1] Mrs Brotherstone was the monthly nurse who attended Princess Beatrice.

sofa, I was always with darling Auntie who you know is the apple of my eye. I went to bed at a few minutes before 7 & slept for 2 hours.

She was moved to the other bed abt. noon wh, was a gt. comfort. Dr Reid gave her the chloroform as he did you. People are all so pleased & I am quite overwhelmed as well as Liko with letters & telegrams.

Will you show this letter with my affectionate love to your Mother-in-law & dear Marie Erbach who both read English or if my hand is illegible, pray copy it for them.

As a rule I like girls best but I *did* wish it shld. be a boy, to be like his dear Father & Uncles, and as I thought it wld be a pleasure to poor dear Sandro in all his trials & troubles.

Pray thank him for his kind, sad letter, as well as your Mother in law for hers – & give my love to Papa, Ludwig, Alicky, Ernie & Franzjos – & my affte. respects to your Father in Law & a kiss to little Alice

Ever your devoted Grandmama

V.R.I.

It is delightful having dear Irène here. I feel so relieved & grateful to God! for having brought dear Auntie safely thro' her gt. troubles, as it lay like a heavy weight hanging over me, for all these months.

During 1886 Victoria's younger sister, Princess Irène of Hesse, and Prince Henry of Prussia (first cousins), had fallen in love and reached an understanding. They had known one another from early childhood, Prince Henry being the second son of Vicky and Fritz, Crown Prince and Princess of Prussia. Henry's elder brother was Prince Wilhelm ('Kaiser Bill') who succeeded his father as Emperor in 1888.

The Queen's relations with her Prussian family were highly unsatisfactory at this time, especially over the Bulgarian business, Germany taking Russia's part.

Once again Queen Victoria's wishes were to be overruled. The young couple married on 24 May 1888. And, once again, the Queen's fears were to be realized. Prince Henry's becoming a Grand Admiral in the German Navy led to many difficulties during Anglo-German naval rivalry, 1898–1914, and the marriage added one more knot to the royal ties with Germany which outraged unwise and ill-informed British public opinion during the First World War.

Princess Irène turned out to be a carrier of haemophilia and passed it on to two of her three sons.

OSBORNE

Feb 2 1887

Darling Victoria,

It is impossible for me to tell you what a shock your letter gave me! Indeed I felt quite ill – for I am so deeply hurt at Irène's conduct *towards me* wh. is neither kind grateful or straightforward. I spoke to her on the subject not long before she left, & said I *don't* say it is never to be, *only don't bind* yourself before he goes away on a long voyage – but say you cannot *as yet* give a promise. And she *assured* me *again* & *again* that she wld. *never do that*! *How can* I trust her again after such conduct? Loving her as I do, treating her & you all as my own Children & having to a gt. extent acted a Mother's part to you all & been so vy intimate with her, this *want* of *openness* has *hurt* me *deeply*. The least she cld. have done wld. be to telegraph *at once to me*: 'Henry is coming after all'. But to *learn* it from the papers *1st*, is too much. I felt such confidence that she wld remain true to her promise to me that I telegraphed *at once* abt. it – in full hope that she *wld* be on her guard!! I am very fond of Henry, but he has behaved *very badly* abt. Sandro & Liko too – & says *very improper* things to his Mother. You say you feel sure I will rejoice at *her happiness*. But that is *just what* I do *not* feel sure of. Henry is not at all strong, the Empress hates *all* connected with your family NOW. Dear Mama did *not* wish such a marriage for any of you, as little as a *Russian* one, & *her wishes* have been totally disregarded. To go into extacies [*sic*] abt. 'Verlobungen' I *never* can. I have seen *so many* unhappy marriages, such crushed & blasted hopes – that I never *can* look but with gt. anxiety upon marriage. Life becomes so full of trials & difficulties in the *happiest* marriage.

I had other *hopes* & *wishes* for Irène, but *my* wishes & hopes seem *never* to be fulfilled so it is useless for me to look forward any more. – I see the advantages wh. possibly may be derived from this union; the very fact that Henry will become the Brother-in-Law of Ludwig who is Brother to Sandro – must have a good influence. I remember now that in speaking to Sandro abt. it & saying how I disliked the idea, he seemed rather to favour it.

You will of course show this letter to Ludwig – & you may also to Ernie. I will write to Irène myself – when I have recd. her 2nd letter. I shall tell her just the same – It reminds me of Ella's & Serge's marriage (wh. I grieve over *as much as ever*) & that *you* were made to announce it to me as (I suspect) *no one* else liked to do it, just after she had *declared* she wld *not* accept him!!

It is too bad to act in that way. I dare hardly hope for better things for lovely Alicky tho' I still have lingering hopes left there!

It made me feel *quite* ill after I had got your letters. The way it has been done, is the worst. Papa & you shld. never have left them together & I fear she was driven into a corner.

I send you an account of a dreadful fright they had at Claremont[1] wh. really makes one's blood run cold! Show it to Papa & 'the others'.

Love to Ludwig & Alicky

Ever your devoted Mama [*sic*]<br>V.R.I.

Queen Victoria was at least as far-sighted as her ministers (and a good deal more percipient than most of them) in her suspicion of Germany's long-term intentions. She regarded Bismarck as a dangerous lunatic and Emperor William I and the Empress as grave threats to the security of Britain and the Empire.

But, having made her protest about Irène's engagement to Prince Henry, the Queen, typically, turns to the practical aspects of the forthcoming marriage: 'Henry must be brought round to a *right* view of things.'

OSBORNE

Feb 15 1887

Darling Victoria,

I have to thank you for your dear letter of the 5th in wh. you explain to me the whole hergang[2] of Irène's very abrupt verlobung. All you say is doubtless true but *still* I *blame* Irène (*after* our *very confidential* talk) *not* writing to *tell me* of Henry's letter to her & hers to him, wh. wld. have somewhat prepared me for what has taken place. This she shld have done & I wish you wld. tell her so.

As regards the marriage itself I *hope* & trust that it may be the means of bringing about a better & more proper & friendly feeling between the 2 Courts – but I *fear* that the *Empress* will *never* be conciliated. She has *never even mentioned* the engagement to Aunt Vicky!! the *Mother* of Henry, wh. is a thing hardly to be understood or believed & she has written most coldly & unkindly to me – in answer to a kind letter of mine!! I send you copies of both & wish dear Papa & Irène to see them both. *I own I* think that during the poor old Empress's life time Irène's position will be very awkward & painful & that therefore the longer the marriage itself is *delayed* the *better*.

The Empress's unkindness is abominable, & considering her former

---

[1] An attempted burglary.
[2] Course of events.

gt. friendship & affection for me it is very painful to see her so vindictive & uncharitable. Louise of Baden has also been most unamiable about it. Irène shld. know all this. I *told* her all this and she seemed then to see it. Hereafter it will doubtless be very different.

I am glad Ella says she is happy but it is the *whole* position in such a *corrupt* Country where you can trust *no one* & where politics are so antagonistic to one's own views & feelings wh. is so sad & distressing to *us* all. Henry must be brought round to a *right* view of things & not become a *2nd* enemy as it were in the midst of the family wh. is too painful. I hope dear Papa will *not* go to the Emperor's birthday & not take poor Irène & expose themselves to *rude treatment* at the Empress's & the Court's hands. Possibly Willie[1] may also be very disagreeable. I don't know what he & what Charlotte have said to it. – I can't *re*-cover [from] the Empress's cold letter. She takes (in the rest of the letter) no *notice* of an allusion I had made to my Jubilee[2] & the threatening clouds in politics. I wonder if she will ignore it altogether.

I hope your Ball will be a gt. success. Do tell Wilhelmina to write a minute acct. of it for me.

Love to Louis – kisses to Baby & love to 'the others'

Ever your devoted Grandmama

V.R.I.

T.O. We go alas! to Windsor on the 22nd.

No sooner had Queen Victoria accepted the inevitability of her grand-daughter Irène's Prussian marriage, than she began to issue warnings and injunctions to Victoria about the last of the Hessian Princesses.

Princess Alix, who bore the worst scars of the family tragedies, was a rather grave, introspective and quite devastatingly beautiful girl. The Queen saw her as the future Queen-Empress of Great Britain and India, married to the Prince of Wales's eldest son, Eddy – and on no account must any Russian come along to 'snap her up'.

[1] Her grandson the future Kaiser Wilhelm II. He often needed a good smacking, the Queen used to say.

[2] The Golden Jubilee celebrations were to take place in June. 'God has sustained me through many great trials and sorrows,' commented the Queen in her Journal.

WINDSOR CASTLE

March 2 1887

Darling Victoria,

We are just starting for London for 3 tiring disagreeable *days* (2 nights) – & I wish to begin my letter with many loving thanks for your 2 of the 22nd & the 26th. Thank God! that our beloved Sandro is going on *now* quite well, but he must have been frightfully ill – & cut off from all – is in itself so cruel & painful. Are the Nurses he had 2 of the Sisters who went to Sofia abt. 14 or 15 months ago? You know Miss Stewart offered to go & nurse him?

As regards your observations respecting Papa's & Irène's going to Berlin, you must let me darling Child speak *very openly*. 1st You always defend those who [are] in the wrong – like the Empress & the spiteful Court of Berlin, & you don't seem to *feel* as you *ought* the insults & indignities put upon dear Papa since 84 – & to your Brother-in-Law.

2ly. I feel very deeply that my opinion & my advice are never listened to & that it is almost useless to give any. – It was not before Ella's marriage was decided on wh. dear Mama wld. never have allowed to come abt. Ella's constant speaking of her happiness I don't quite like. *When* people are very happy they don't require to *tell* others of it.

As Irène has been lost to us here – I must tell you, who have so much influence with Papa & generally in the family, that my heart & mind are bent on securing dear Alicky for either Eddie or Georgie. You must prevent *further* Russians or other people *coming* to snap her up.

Ludwig says the Prussian is the best Protestant Parti, *apart* from affection – I say England is better. And I hope to *live* to *see* one of darling Mama's girls here. But when Irène & perhaps you *for a time too* – are gone she *must not* be *left* to Miss Jackson *alone*, with her bad health, hard ways & crabbed, bad temper. It wld ruin Alicky. Some one must be found for her, younger, softer, brighter, else her life all alone will be utterly miserable. It should be someone like Fr. Fabrice[1] who is with the S. Holstein cousins, such a very nice person; she has several sisters one of whom might do. Pray thank Ludwig very much for his long letter – & the charming Sketches – several of wh. will be executed. I think it wld. hardly do to have any of them made at Darmstadt on the present occasion.

How frightful these earthquakes[2] have been! Have you heard anything of Herr Muther since he left?

We stop here till the day after tomorrow when we return to Windsor. We shall be coming up again on the 17th for my 2nd Drawing room. I

---

[1] This governess left the Schleswig-Holstein family for Hesse in December.

[2] Northern Italy and the south of France were beset by heavy earthquakes in 1887.

am so glad dear little Alice enjoyed her birthday. With earnest prayers for the speedy recovery of dear Sandro, believe me ever.

Your devoted Grandmama<br>V.R.I.

In the early summer of 1887 Victoria caught typhoid and became very ill. Her husband, deeply concerned, helped to look after her. 'There never was so kind a nurse,' Victoria noted. There seemed little chance of her being well enough to attend her grandmother's Golden Jubilee celebrations. But, almost at the last minute, Victoria was able to give the Queen better news.

BALMORAL CASTLE

June 10 1887

Darling Victoria,

I cannot say with what joy I received your dear little pencil Note & what thankfulness to God fills my heart for your preservation through this horrid illness! You have been most tenderly loving [*sic*] nursed by one of the kindest & best of Husbands whose love & unbounded devotion you can never sufficiently repay. The hope & I trust I may say, *certain* hope, of seeing you after all at my Jubilee is an immense pleasure, but you must *not* attempt more than that. *No* dinner parties or Parties – but you shld. go quietly down to Windsor on the mng. of the 22nd to meet on that evg. or afternoon when my Statue is unveiled at the foot of the Castle Hill.

And then I hope you will remain with us there till we go to Osborne when you wld go to Albert Cottage.

Ever your devoted Grandmama<br>V.R.I.

T.O.   We have had *all* the time excepting 2 or 3 days at 1st such splendid, bright warm weather & all so forward & green & full of flowers – & in England it has been cold & wet.

BALMORAL CASTLE

Aug 26 1887

Darling Victoria,

On this ever dear day,[1] once so bright & joyous & *still* joyful in a reflected manner to me, I write to thank you for your last dear letter & to send you these Photos: of me in *my* Jubilee Dress – for you, dear Papa & darling Ernie – who I hope to hear more from again.

[1] The Prince Consort's birthday.

I am sure you must miss dear Ludwig,[1] one of the kindest & best of Husbands, very much, tho' you rejoice in his being again employed. Uncle Affie[2] writes they (and Georgie) had an excellent passage out, & that Ludwig was delighted with his Ship. – We have found as hot weather here as we left at Osborne. The separation from At Vicky was very sad, but still sadder from dear Uncle Arthur – for so long to come. Have just heard from him fr. Suez & he is now in the Red Sea.

At. Louischen's leg is so much better for her cure at Aix which is still going on.

How much fatigue I have had & how much has been going on ever since you left, dear Sisters will have told you. They are very well. Dear Auntie Beatrice bore the journey wonderfully well – & is glad to feel she need not move again before the gt. Event[3] is over wh. will I think be at the end of September or beginning of October – but of course might, as last time, come a little sooner.

Dear little Baby cut his *1st* tooth in the Train. How is sweet Baby Alice? Give my kindest love to your Parents in Law & dear Sandro, & believe [unfinished]

Following the exhausting Golden Jubilee celebrations, the Queen suffered another savage blow in the death of 'my darling old Noble'. She sent two photographs of the dog to Victoria and commented: 'It is indeed a grievous loss to me of a *real* friend whom I miss terribly.' Victoria joined her husband in Malta in October 1887. She formed a great affection for the island, on which she lived frequently when Louis was serving in the Mediterranean Fleet.

The Crown Prince of Prussia was at this time causing great anxiety with a throat infection which turned out to be cancer. His father died on 9 March 1888 and was succeeded as German Emperor by his gravely ill son. His reign lasted just ninety-nine days, Wilhelm II succeeding him at the age of twenty-nine. The new young Emperor mistreated his mother, the Queen's eldest daughter, atrociously. There was no love lost between the British and German courts.

[1] Prince Louis had been appointed Commander (Executive Officer) of the new ironclad *Dreadnought* in the Mediterranean.

[2] Prince Alfred had hoisted his flag in the battleship *Alexandra* in the Mediterranean. Prince George served also in the flagship.

[3] Princess Beatrice's second child, later the Queen of Spain.

*To*

*dear Victoria & Ludwig Battenberg*

*from*

*their loving*

*Grandmama*

*Victoria R.S.*

*Christmas - 1887. ——*

OSBORNE

2 Jan 1888

Darling Victoria,

Only today can I wish you a happy New Year, wh. I do with all my heart. God bless & protect you darling, dear Ludwig & sweet little Alice, for many many years. I am very glad that you like Malta & find it so pleasant – tho' doubtless Papa Sisters & Ernie are often thought of. – I feel quite shocked to find how long it is since I wrote! I cld. not believe it & I find I have never thanked you (unless I did not mark it down – as I do all my letters) for your letters of the 19th Oct: 2nd Nov: & 14th Dec!! wh. is quite shocking besides of course the 2 last dear ones of the 19th & 26th Dec. Your descriptions of your voyage & your life at Malta are very vivid & enable me to follow *all* in thought. – The blessed improvement in dear Uncle Fritz's throat & in his general health is a source of unspeakable happiness to us! Indeed it cheered us all at Christmas & New Year both of wh. days are very sad for me now, since *first* the 14th of Dec *61* & then again in *78* – & other sad losses wh. are felt very *forcibly* on such days.

The darling little Connaughts were much missed on Christmas Eve but little Alice & Charlie were here both very merry, good & obedient Children – & the former very pretty – & darling little Drino was delighted carried in good Mahomed's[1] arms. They are devoted to one another, & I never saw a more careful Nurse than Mahomed is.

I am so thankful that it has at last been satisfactorily arranged abt. Miss Jackson, & Fr. v. Fabrice who I think is just the right person for dear Alicky.

I fancy Irène's marriage[2] is to take place in May at Potsdam wh. I am very sorry for – but wh. I certainly shld. not *any how* have been present at except at Darmstadt, & in May it is *quite* impossible for me to go abroad again – as we are going D.V. in March – to *Florence* – where the Dow<sup>r</sup> Lady Crawford has lent us a beautiful Villa of hers 2 miles out of the Town & wh. she had offered to us several times already.

It must be very nice for you to see so much of dear Aunt Marie & Uncle Affie & those dear Children, & very nice for them too, to see much of you.

Dear Auntie is very well & strong & looking very well, & the Babies are charming, little Victoria Ena reminds me so much of the Photographs of Ella as a Baby & of Alicky also. But Auntie *must* have a very long rest.

And now asking again your pardon for not writing for so long – (wh.

[1] Her Indian servant. The Queen was taking lessons in Hindustani, from Abdul Karim, at this time.

[2] She married Prince Henry at Charlottenburg on 24 May 1888.

I cld hardly help – for I have not got over my arrears yet, & am very much overworked & very tired) & thanking Ludwig for his very kind letter.

Believe me always your devoted Grandmama<br>V.R.I.

I *do* hope we shall meet in this New strange year of *three 8's* – There are to be Tableaux here Twelfth Night (6th). Tuxen's[1] picture is beautiful

BALMORAL CASTLE

June 14 1888

Darling Child,

I am so distressed not to have written for so long & you have written such dear, charming letters to me, wh. have given me great pleasure. Many thanks now for your dear letters of the 18th Ap: 12th 20th & 27th of May – as well as for the beautiful & most curious Shell, & the very pretty Drawing of one of my favourite Gipsies.

Auntie Beatrice came back delighted at her stay at Jugenheim, – & at the gt. kindness of her Parents-in-Law & Geschwister.

Alas! since the last 3 or 4 days – after having improved so much – dear Uncle Fritz has again been dreadfully ill[2] & the day before yesterday we feared the worst at every moment! Thank God! & wonderful to say, he is again a little better & able to take some nourishment, & to be out.

As you have so lately had a confidential conversation with W.[3] (wh. Auntie showed me your account of) in wh. he spoke bitterly of his poor Mother, I beg you to entreat him to let bygones be bygones & especially not to let *that* one subject wh. was dreadful, affect his kindness towards her *otherwise*, and above all to show every attention to her *wishes* concerning *sad things* wh. wld. have to be done if the *worst happened*. Tell him that the more respect he shows to her & his father & the more consideration for her wishes, the more he will be liked by his Country & *all* of *us*. – The reverse wld do *him* immense harm. You can say this best as he trusts you. I have written very kindly to him & also *hinted* at it, in thanking him for his birthday letter to me.

We have had the most unsettled & disappointing Spring Season here – I ever remember.

I am so disappointed that dear Ella cld not come over for a little bit.

---

[1] Lauritz Tuxen, a Danish artist who painted a Jubilee picture of the Royal Family.

[2] He died the next day.

[3] By the time this letter was received Wilhelm was Emperor.

How seldom she comes away from that Exile, & how different to what we hoped & believed. When exactly will dear Papa, Alicky & Ernie come? It is nonsense to say they shld go to another bathing place for the bathing at Osborne & in the Isle of Wight generally is quite excellent – & then (for Alicky) a good long stay with us here wh. wld. be delightful wld do her the gst. good.

I am so distressed to hear that dear Ludwig had a return of fever at Malta.[1]

Trusting dear little Alice is well.

Ever your devoted Mama [*sic*]<br>V.R.I.

WINDSOR CASTLE

July 4 1888

Darling Victoria,

Auntie B. has already thanked you for your letter of the 29th & told you that I entirely approve it, & so does Uncle Bertie. – It is however sad that poor dear Auntie V.[2] who is so utterly broken hearted shld have this additional gt. grief for it *will* be that, & I dread what may happen. But *still* it *had to be done*.

I hope that Ernie & Alicky will arrive abt. the 1st or 2nd Aug: as we must leave on the 21st to go to Glasgow. When wld. Papa arrive?

It is too dreadful for us all to think of Willy & Bismarck & Dona[3] – being the supreme head of all now! Two so unfit & one so wicked. He spoke so shamefully about dear Auntie V. to Uncle Bertie &. At. Alix

I hope Fr: v. Fabrice is giving satisfaction? & gets on well with Alicky? I must end to write to At Vicky.

You will I am sure be shocked to hear (if you have not already heard it) of poor, good Mrs Profeit's[4] very sad & sudden death on the 25th. She was going to have her 10th Child in a month & was very nervous & low abt it being very delicate. She went to bed fairly well on the night of the 25th (we had seen her on the 19th) & woke with a sensation of choking. They gave her some whisky & water; but the choking returned & she said 'I am dying'. They put her into bed again, in 10 m. *all*

---

[1] Malta Fever was a debilitating illness often suffered by the Navy in the Mediterranean. It was eventually traced to the unclean teats of the island's goats whose milk was widely drunk.

[2] The Dowager Empress of Germany.

[3] 'Willy's' wife, 'Dona' now the German Empress, a weak-willed woman who quite failed to stem the Kaiser's excesses.

[4] Wife of the Commissioner at Balmoral, Dr Alexander Profeit.

was *over*! The poor Doctor is quite broken down & so are the poor Children.

Pray tell Papa & the others of her sad death. She will be terribly missed. It was heart.

Love to all. Ever your devoted Mama [*sic*]

V.R.I.

BALMORAL CASTLE

Oct 2 1888

Darling Victoria,

I was long intending to thank you for your dear letter of the 10th from Kiel wh. gave me such pleasure as it gives such a pleasant account of darling Irène's new Home & the people etc. But I had meant to write also to tell you how *utterly* incapable I am of expressing my deep sorrow & distress at this dreadful new misfortune wh. is impending & of the same horrible & (till *now*) *not* curable malady – wh. has attacked your dear, kind charming Father in Law.[1] When I got your dear letter of the 29th yesterday I assure you it makes me *quite miserable*, & I do feel so distressed for you all, and you know *how* devoted I am to the *whole charming family*. Really I *can't* find words to say what I feel – & always will *hope* it may not be so bad. *This* illness is one wh. I think *justifies every attempt* to *arrest* the progress & *relieve* the *pain* & I *know* of many cases – in wh. *Mather's* medicines & outward applications have caused great relief & can do no harm. I am asking after them now, & will send them, as they are harmless.

Also P. Ennarets [?] has a remedy wh. is said to be wonderful. *He* wished dear Uncle Fritz to try it – as he knew several instances where pain is gtly diminished & life *prolonged*, for several years, so that one person died of *something quite* different. The Doctors are very obstinate & don't like anything to be tried, but I *entreat & implore* you, to use every possible thing wh. cld. prolong so precious a life & relieve pain. He could be told it was for Geschwüre.[2]

I feel so much for dear Ludwig & our poor dear Liko, whom we try to cheer. – Surely *if* his dear father is so ill Ludwig cannot leave him & *you cld* not go?

Darling Alicky who is dear & good & clever has, I am sure, told you everything of our life here.

Auntie (who is very much devoted to your father-in-law & is grtly distressed) has just recovered from a bad cold wh. fell on her chest – from a little neglect at first – The way poor dear Aunt Vicky is persecuted & attacked & the way in wh. those vile Bismarcks & *their crew*

---

[1] Prince Alexander was mortally ill and died on 15 December 1888.
[2] Ulcers.

attack her & dear Uncle's memory is not to be borne! But es wird sich rächen! [1] Does dear Papa *know abt.* dear Pce Alex*er*?

Willy has behaved most outrageously to Uncle Bertie.

Now I must end, Ever your devoted Grandmama

V.R.I.

T.O. A kiss to little Alice. I *do so* feel for your dear Mother-in-law.

Queen Victoria's interest, which sometimes approached obsessive proportions, in dates, coincidences and anniversaries, is shown again in this first letter of the year of her own seventieth birthday. She had often remarked on the three '8s' of the previous year; now she remarks not only on coincidental anniversaries, but even near-anniversaries!

OSBORNE

Jan 5 1889

Darling Victoria,

Many loving thanks for your dear affte. letters of the 22nd & 29th. Christmas was to all of us a very sad time, & how strange & mysterious that with only a few hours difference, your dear Father-in-law & Great Uncle[2] shld have been taken from us all at the same time of year, – that dreadful month of Dec: wh. took away your beloved Mama, & 17 years before, dear Grandpapa & wh. so nearly carried off Uncle Bertie in 71! It seems as though there was in this, the bond of sorrow (wh. is far stronger than that of joy) a new tie between our families wh. are already so much linked together!

What a journey you must have had & what harrowing scenes you witnessed & wh. I am sure none of you will ever forget! Ludwig has indeed the same comfort wh. dear GdPapa had when his Father died – & far away – that he had never caused his Father any sorrow.

Do *all* you can to help & comfort your poor Mama-in-law who is the one most to be pitied & felt for. Dear Auntie feels it very deeply, as having no Father of her own, she loved your dear Father-in-law *very much. Those* 4 days were terrible, but she is none the worse. Is it not *too* bad, *too* hard & provoking – that she shld again be expecting another Child!![3] I told Ludwig what I felt. It spoils the whole Spring.

[1] 'He won't get away with it.'

[2] Prince Alexander of Hesse was her great uncle as well as her father-in-law.

[3] Princess Beatrice's son Prince Leopold of Battenberg (1889–1922), later Lord Leopold Mountbatten.

I quite understand what you say abt. dear Papa's going to Berlin for the New Year & occasionally but I wish Papa wld tell Henry he must really refuse to be called constantly away from darling Irène in her present state;[1] it might do her serious harm. I think heartless W. [Kaiser Wilhelm] wishes to keep them apart for fear of her getting a good influence over Henry.

I hope dear little Alice [no ending]

WINDSOR CASTLE

Feb 20 1889

Darling Victoria,
So many thanks for your 2 dear letters of the 9th & the 17th.

I am delighted to hear that you have been to Kiel to see poor darling Irène whom I hope you have found well. I hear that Ludwig was most kindly & civilly recd. at Copenhagen wh. is very gratifying but it could not be otherwise as the King is so good & kind & was so fond of your dear Father-in-law & Uncle.

I grieve for you that the *Event*[2] (wh. I rejoice at, as I think an *only* Child is such an anxiety besides being bad for the Child herself) – shld take place at the hottest time of year & when your hay fever is so bad & it is so dreadfully hot & the gnats are so bad at Jugenheim.

– Since I began this letter I have seen Mrs Paterson[3] who is a nice strong comfortable person, *well* up in her profession & very kindly. She is prepared to go back by Darmstadt when she leaves darling Irène wh. I suppose wld not be for a month or perhaps more after the Event takes place to see you. She is quite free on the 1st of July. I have told her to get everything that is required wh. you have *not* got.

The death of the C. Pce of Austria[4] is too horrible. There is *no doubt whatever* but that he led a very bad life, & that this unfortunate girl said to be one of the prettiest & I *fear* fastest in Vienna *Mlle. Marie Vetsera* only 19 – was found *dead, on his bed, both dead*, & shot – & a pistol in his hand. She was said to be very exaltée[5] & wrote to her Mother the day before she went to Mayerling that she would be dead next day!! Several people I fear have helped in their guilty affair – & none more than the Empress's own niece, Ctss. Larisch[6] who owes everything to the

[1] She was carrying Prince Waldemar of Prussia (1889–1945).

[2] The birth of Princess Louise. (See footnote 2, page 103.)

[3] A monthly nurse.

[4] The scandal at Mayerling; the double suicide/murder of Rudolph, Crown Prince of Austria, and Mademoiselle Vetsera.

[5] Ardent.

[6] Marie Larisch, daughter of the morganatic marriage of Prince Rudolph's mother's brother and Countess Wallersee.

Empress. The poor, poor Emperor & the Empress are gtly to be pitied
– for it is awful altogether. Poor Stephanie[1] was not happy I fear, for
some years past & though the *loss to her* will not be as great, the horror
of the whole thing, & the impossibility of having any respect or love
for her dead Husband must leave an awful impression & be most painful to her!

How is your dear Mother-in-law?

My poor darling Beatrice is much to be pitied but I am really very
angry about it – for it is very bad for her, a useless expense & a gt
annoyance & inconvenience to me, deranging all my usual & (for my
health most necessary) arrangements.[2]

I am sending today a 'dolly' for dear little Alice's birthday & a hot
dish will follow.

And now I must end, with a very kind remembrance to your dear
Mother-in-law & love to Ludwig

Ever your devoted Grandmama<br>V.R.I.

Dear Auntie is unberufen very well & her Children delightful & the
gtst possible darlings.

Dear At. Vicky & the dear girls, alas! leave us on the 26th (we get
to Town on the 25th to the 27th) & on the 25th [*sic*] we start for
Biarritz.

PAVILLON LA ROCHEFOUCAULD, BIARRITZ

March 31 1889

Darling Victoria,

Let me 1st say *how* delighted I am at darling Irène's safety & the birth
of a boy – though a girl would perhaps have been better when there are
already so many Princes who will stand in one another's way. But this
one is much more likely to be *nice* & perhaps to be a comfort to poor At
Vicky. Dear Irène had such a wonderfully quick time. She was only
*really* 3 hours ill – & the first symptoms began in the night – When I
think of you & how long you were ill, a whole night & day in such
severe pain! I hope *this* time you will *not* have much trouble. Dr Champneys is as clever as Dr Williams who attended Auntie & particularly

---

[1] Prince Rudolph's wife, formerly Princess of Belgium and daughter of
Leopold II.

[2] Prince Henry ('Liko') of Battenberg had paid a heavy price for the hand
of Princess Beatrice and had found himself very confined in his activities and
movements, dearly though he may have been devoted to the Queen. He proposed to go shooting in Albania – 'a very foolish expedition' commented the
Queen.

nice & gentleman-like. – His father was a Dean & his wife is the daughter of a Baronet. I shall see him before he goes – & I suppose he shld be at Darmstadt by the end of June?

Let me now thank you for your dear letter of the 9th & another soon after (I have mislaid it for the moment & don't remember the date). I am so glad you liked the presents for sweet little Alice.

Oh! dear Sandro! it is a sad thing – especially that he did it[1] without saying one word to any one of his Brothers & in such a hurry!

I hope & trust that your poor dear Mother-in-law will be the better for the change & quiet she has determined to have tho' it rather startles one! May God help & soothe her poor troubled heart & mind. I am sure in time all will look less gloomy to her.

And now let me say a word about Alicky. Is there *no* hope abt. E.?[2] She is *not* 19 – & she shld. be made to reflect seriously on the folly of throwing away the chance of a very good Husband, kind, affectionate & steady & of entering a united happy family & a very good position wh. is second to *none* in *the world*! Dear Uncle & Aunt wish it so much & poor E. is so unhappy at the thought of losing her also! Can you & Ernie not do any good? What fancy has she got in her head?

We like this place very much tho the scenery is not as fine as Aix excepting for the magnificent sea wh. in the storms of wind & rain we had yesterday & the Evg. before was splendid; the line of the Pyrenees too is very fine only distant & the drives towards the Mountains are lovely. We have had some very warm weather & some very cold, & a good deal of bright weather tho' not as much as I expected. The air is delicious, so light & strengthening. Poor darling Auntie is unberufen wonderfully well & enjoying it very much. Aunt Louise & Uncle Lorne came here yesterday for 2 or 3 days from Arcachon.

You & Ludwig will grieve over the sad loss of the poor 'Sultan'[3] wh. has distressed Uncle A. very much. And now I will end my long letter – asking you to write to me more especially abt. A. –

Love to Ludwig & Alicky & Ernie & thanks for his letter, & a kiss to Baby.

                                   Ever your devoted old Grandmama
                                                            V.R.I.

[1] Ex-Prince Alexander of Battenberg, foiled by Bismarck in his attempt to marry Princess Victoria of Prussia, married morganatically an Austrian opera singer, Johanna Loisinger.

[2] The Queen was still hoping, against all the evidence, that Princess Alix of Hesse might accept her grandson, Prince Albert Victor (Eddie).

[3] This battleship, in which Affie and Louis had served together, sank after striking a rock in the Comino Channel, Malta, on 6 March, but was salvaged and survived until 1947 as a hulk.

We are going on the 27th to San Sebastian to meet the Queen Regent[1] of Spain. And on the 2nd we intend to leave Biarritz

ON BOARD THE V. & ALBERT NEAR PORTRUSH

April 1 1889

Darling Victoria,

These lines are to wish you many, *many happy* returns of your dear birthday[2] wh however I fear will be somewhat saddened by the thought of your dear Father-in-law's loss & of your poor dear Sandro whom we & *I* in particular wld wish to telegraph my good wishes to – as of old – only where to? Would Ludwig try to do so for me?

If he had *only* had a little patience!

May *every* blessing be yours for *many* & *many* a year to come.

We have had a quick & rolling passage from a ground swell – but Auntie (who is unberufen wonderfully strong & well as well as I much benefitted by our stay at Biarritz) was not very ill & I – *not the least* ill only we laid down & kept quiet. I think Capt. Fullerton anticipated a worse passage.

Darling Irène is going on very well but very slowly! Aunt Vicky & Mrs Paterson are bent on keeping her in bed for a long time & she is (vainly I suspect) trying to nurse. You must *not* submit to be kept *in* bed for a fortnight & more – wh. no one dreams of here. I hear your Event is not to come off till the *end* of July! wh. is a month later than was 1st expected, is it not?

I am very anxious to hear from you in answer – as I don't know else what to do abt. dear Papa's & Alicky's coming to England on acct. of the latter's behaviour abt. Eddy.

We enjoyed our stay at Biarritz very much tho' excepting for a brilliant sun & with the exception of a few very warm days – at the very beginning & in the middle of [our] stay, it was cold & the trees leafless!! Still camellias were blooming in profusion, mimosas – quantities of violets all in the open air – & many wild flowers, there are also splendid large magnolia trees! It was an unusually cold & backward season they say. There is a gt. deal of historical interest everywhere, & the country reminds me of the Isle of Wight. The scenery, the mountains [Pyrenees] wh. in clear weather you see very distinctly – is beautiful, & the sea magnificent. The peasants [Basques] are simple, kind good & most civil people – & so kind to us; handsome people – tall & dark & such beautiful Children. I can't say really – how extraordinarily kind & civil & empressé the French high & low – beginning with the Authorities are

[1] Maria Christina, widow of King Alfonso XII of Spain.
[2] Her twenty-sixth.

Page from the Heilgenberg visitors' book on the Queen's 70th birthday. The second Victoria was the Empress Frederick, and Sophie was her daughter who married King Constantine I of Greece, brother of Andrew, who married Victoria's daughter Alice.

to me & *us*. Nothing cld exceed it anywhere. And wherever we went all the people & children crying 'Viva la Reina'. This is in fact Spanish. Our visit to San Sebastian was most interesting & striking & the Queen Regent is *quite* charming.

Tell all I have told you to dear Papa, who *never* writes any more! His last letter only spoke of dinners & balls & nothing else. – What terrible catastrophes the German Navy & *Colonial* proceedings have suffered!

Love to Ludwig

Ever your devoted Grandmama

V.R.I.

T.O.

*Do* write to me abt. poor Abby.[1] How is your poor dear Mother-in-law? I hope my picture will please you.

Willy, now German Emperor, paid a visit to England with Prince Bismarck in July–August 1889, and attended the Naval Review at Spithead. He made the Queen Colonel-in-Chief of the 1st Dragoon Guards, and the Queen (reluctantly) made him an Admiral in the British Navy, an honour he had for long coveted.

OSBORNE

Aug 7 1889

Darling Victoria,

Your dear letter of the 3rd has given me very great pleasure. I am so thankful all is well over,[2] but grieve that you again suffered so much.

If Dr Champneys had only arrived in time I am sure you wld have suffered less!

I am very glad you like Mrs Paterson she is a good Nurse, & a sensible woman, I have always heard.

The visit *here* is going off quite well – tho' it is very hard to have to swallow that horrid Herbert B.[3] who everyone dislikes – & that Traitor Kessell. Willy is quite amiable; he is grown very large & puffed in the face. He seems pleased with everything. Henry is always kind & good natured & devoted to your dear Irène.

On Monday evg I recd the Deputation from the Regt. of wh. Willy very kindly has made me Chief – a very distinguished Regt. in wh.

[1] Prince Albert of Schleswig-Holstein.
[2] The birth of Princess Louise on 13 July.
[3] Bismarck, Prussian Foreign Minister.

beloved Uncle Fritz served himself. Willy introduced them & made a very pretty speech & I *had* to say something in return.

We dine in the large Tent just as at Auntie's wedding.

I am sure the dear Baby for whose Christening I send many good wishes will be very pretty.

I will send you Photos of Louise & McDuff[1] & the Chapel; I send you an acct. today.

That Alicky & Ernie are coming so soon, I am delighted at. If only poor Eddy (who is so devoted to Alicky) I felt had decided what to do or not to do abt. Alicky I wish so much to know.

Love to Ludwig & thanks for his letter.

Ever your devoted Grandmama<br>V.R.I.

Auntie is very well & Baby weighed 12 lbs at 2 months.


BALMORAL CASTLE
Oct 12 1889

Darling Victoria,

I have never thanked you for your last dear letter wh. I do now. You will, I hope, not have been frightened by dear Ludwig's most untoward accident, caused 1st by getting his foot in a hole, – out stalking & then by some very unnecessary dancing[2] after the Performance wh. was so very successful. However it improved wonderfully – for it was a severe sprain, & he was able to go to London yesterday, but he will have to be very careful for a long time & ought to wear an elastic sock.

We have heard that he bore the journey to London quite well. He will have told you everything & Ernie & Alicky also.

It is most sad abt. Alicky & Eddie. We have still a faint, lingering hope that she *may* – if he remains unmarried, after all when she comes to reflect & see *what* a sad & serious thing it is to throw away such a marriage with such a position, & in such an amiable family in her Mother's country – where she wld be received with open arms – & change. Moreover Eddie is not stupid, is very good, affectionate & a good looking young man.

I am glad to hear Irène is weaning the Baby. It is high time she shld as it is such a big Child I hear.

It is so sad that your dear Mother-in-law is still so unwell. If she wld leave Darmstadt for a little change it wld be so good.

[1] The Princess of Wales's eldest daughter, Princess Louise, married to the Earl (later Duke) of Fife.

[2] There was no such thing as 'unnecessary' dancing in the eyes of Prince Louis, who adored it. But it was a nasty sprain.

I hope the dear Children are well? Alice, I hear, is lovelier than ever. Little Drino & Ena[1] are quite delightful – so amusing.

I regret Irène only coming to us in May. It will be more than two years & a half since I have seen her! And when shall I see you?

Dear Ernie I found as dear & childlike as ever but so sensible right-minded & clever.

With love to Papa & 'the others'.

Ever your devoted Grandmama
V.R.I.

BALMORAL CASTLE
Oct 30 1889

Darling Child,

Many, many thanks for your dear letters of the 14th & 17th with the pretty tho' not well arranged photograph of yourself, Ludwig & Family.

The likenesses are charming & I hear that little Louise is very pretty. It will be a terrible separation for you from them I fear, but it is much wiser not to take them, besides they will be a gt. comfort to your poor, lonely Mother-in-law who, I hope is better? I *do* feel *so much* for her.

It is a gt. relief for us to know dear Ludwig safely arrived[2] & I hope the foot nearly well. I wonder what sort of passage he had.

We have just a *faint lingering* hope that Alicky *might in time* look to see what a pleasant home, & what a *useful* position she will lose if she ultimately *persists* in not yielding to Eddy's *really earnest* wishes. He wrote to me he shld. *not* give up the idea (tho' it is considered for the *present at an end*) – and: 'I don't think she knows how I love her, or she cld. not be so cruel.'

There are so few for her to marry & Eddie is *very* good! However if after he returns[3] – improved & developped [*sic*] as we *must hope* he will be – *who cld* he marry? *Do* tell me.[4]

Liko is soon leaving us on what *I* consider a very foolish expedition & I hope he wont be very long away & come back safe. Aunt Lily wld not like it if Pawel remained very long absent. – I will now end, begging you just to telegraph your safe arrival at Malta. When does Irène follow you? Every one says her boy is so fine & big.

[1] Princess Beatrice's children, Alexander and Victoria Eugénie.

[2] Prince Louis had returned, still with foot trouble, to Malta.

[3] From a visit to India.

[4] Prince Albert Victor became engaged to Princess Mary ('May') of Teck on 3 December 1891. She was the daughter of the Queen's first cousin, the Duchess of Teck.

Poor Calma[1] has a 4th daughter!

With kisses to little Alice & many loves to Papa (who I hope will visit us this winter) & Alicky & kindest remembrances to your poor Mother-in-law.

Ever your devoted Grandmama
V.R.I.

From the year 1890 the last tragedy of Queen Victoria's much-loved Hessian grand-daughters was played out. It is evident from earlier letters that the Queen had been for some time harbouring dread suspicions that little Alicky would 'go to horrid Russia'. Four more years were to pass before her fears were finally realized with Alicky's engagement to the Tsarevitch, 'Nicky' (the Queen spelt him 'Niki'), the eldest son of Emperor Alexander III, at the wedding at Coburg of Ernie to his first cousin 'Ducky' – Princess Victoria Melita, Affie's daughter.

Much agonizing heartsearching, accusation and counter-accusation still lay ahead, and in 1890 the whole hideous question of Alicky's future loomed large in Queen Victoria's mind – and correspondence – for a further four years.

WINDSOR CASTLE
July 15 1890

Darling Victoria,

I will write to you today instead of to dear Papa & ask you to answer his questions.

1st. He misunderstood me a little when I said that I regretted Alicky's again going to Russia as it led to every sort of report – but I did not mean that it meant anything abt. Niki as he is away & besides it wld. not do on acct. of the religion, & I know moreover Minnie[2] does not *wish* it. In short *that* cld *not* be. But there are many other Grand dukes & Pces: & I heard that Ella was determined to try & get a marriage with another Russian & *this* I meant wld. grievously hurt Uncle Bertie & At Alix as well *as me*. But it may not be true, & if you take care & *tell* Ella that no marriage for *Alicky in Russia* wld be *allowed*, then there will be *an end of it*; But I am afraid reports will be spread again. Do you bring Ella back with you?

[1] Princess Caroline Matilda, wife of the Duke of Schleswig-Holstein.
[2] See footnote 1, page 110.

We are very anxious for Ernie to pay us a visit. I hope he will come to Scotland when we are there, that always does him so much good.

I hope the Children are well & Baby quite recovered & that she has got some teeth? I hope that little Alice's deafness is better?

I feel a good deal lost without dear Auntie Beatrice. She left to-morrow week-ago, & is making a very nice Tour & goes on to Oberammergau. The dear Children are with me & unberufen v well & funny.

Dear Aunt Vicky & both girls are leaving this evng from here embarking on the Yacht from Portsmouth at 7 & go on at once hoping to reach Gibraltar on Sunday eveng or Monday Mng – I shall be fidgety till I hear they have arrived safely. And then they must go on in the Surprise[1] (to Corfu I suppose) & Athens. Vicky[2] was not to have gone but as her marriage already takes place in Nov: neither she or her Mama wld like to be separated for so long. We like Adolf extremely & he is very good looking amiable & sensible. But of course she cannot feel the *same* as she did for Sandro. That was a *passion* & *1st* attachment. Still I think she will be happy & make a good wife. He is *very* fond of her.

Sir Wm. White[3] asked very much after Ludwig. I am sorry that he has to go to Suakim as it is so hot there but he can keep away from the coast a good deal & not go on shore.

Uncle Affie & At Marie & all the children (who are charming & the two eldest girls very handsome & looking quite grown up) are in England, the children are now with me. They are (the girls) very pretty strong & healthy & dear, good children admirably brought up; they will make excellent *partis*[4] some day. Young Alfred is a dear good boy, too.

We go the day after tomorrow to Osborne & Aunt Lenchen is going with us till the 28th.

Dear Aunt Vicky keeps talking & I must close in a hurry having just seen her off. This is the 5th day without rain & the 2nd really hot summers day, I must end – I am so sorry poor dear Irène has had to be pulled abt. but please God she will get quite well again.

I hope your dear Mother-in-law is better?

Ever your devoted Grandmama

V.R.I.

---

[1] C.-in-C.'s Despatch Vessel.

[2] She married Prince Adolphus of Schaumburg-Lippe on the recoil from Sandro.

[3] The notable naval architect.

[4] Matches.

By the close of 1890, the ageing Queen recognized two related and harsh truths – that darling Alicky was 'lost' to her, and that one reason for this was the conduct of Alicky's older sister, Ella, now married to Grand Duke Serge for six years and anxious to have one of her sisters near her. After much heartsearching, Ella had renounced her religion, and been received into the Greek Orthodox Church. She was to persuade Princess Alix that it was not such a terrible experience, that in fact the two religions had much in common.


BALMORAL CASTLE
                                              Oct 15 1890
Darling Victoria,
   It was an age since I had heard from you & I was very pleased to receive your dear letter of the 26th Sept. from Illinskoe[1] where I am glad to see you spent such a pleasant time. You are now soon leaving for Malta[2] where I hope you & the children will all keep well. I feel very much for your poor dear Mother-in-law having to lose the dear Children & to spend a winter so *alone*!
   We have had a very *gay* autumn. Splendid warm summer ever since the 2nd of Sept. with but few stormy or colder days occasionally between – but not *one* night's *frost*. The leaves have only turned within the last week & we still had strawberries a few days ago! The excellent Band wh. Fife has every year at Mar, came here for a fortnight & played every evng with an *entrain* I never heard in any English band before! – Then we had *very* successful Tableaux during & between wh. the Band played. I enclose the Program wh. please give to Alicky whom we thought so much of! – I hope *still* to see her & Ernie before the end of the year! It is the 1st time *since 11 years* that *none* of you have been here with me!! I hope I was *right* in telling Uncle Bertie that I *knew* there was *no question* of a *Marriage* for *her in Russia*, & that you have brought her back safe & *free*? Uncle Bertie says he knows Ella will move Heaven & Earth to get her to marry a Gd. duke!
   Now with many loves to all,
                                      Ever your devoted Grandmama
                                                    V.R.I.


   [1] Grand Duke Serge and Ella's country home near Moscow.
   [2] Victoria was returning to Malta but her husband was at sea. He had recently been given his first command, H.M.S. *Scout*, a torpedo-cruiser.

OSBORNE

Darling Victoria,                                    Dec 19 1890

Your dear letter of the 24th Nov: gave me great pleasure, especially the hope of seeing you D.V. next year. Would it be direct from Malta (by Brindisi) early in May or later? Please say. I wish you a very happy Christmas tho' it will be sad without dear Ludwig, & also *many many* happy years. I hope you will like my present for your writing table & use it, & that the presents for the sweet little girlies will also be acceptable. I enclose a Card for you, for Alice, one for Louis for New Year wh. please forward & one for Victoria (Moretta)[1] & Adolf *together*.

I want to write to you a longish letter abt. Alicky but find I cannot do it *tonight*. – We came here today – & I was very glad to leave Windsor where we have lived for 4 weeks in frost, some very severe ones, & for a week in thick fogs & awful darkness.

Auntie B. had a feverish cold wh. kept her in bed nearly for a week from the 9th till the 14th & in her room till the 16th. She is quite well again but rather weak still. I have had a slight cold in my head the last few days – but it is nothing & I was never kept in doors. – A terribly sad thing happened on the 12th. Good Sir E. Böhm the greatest living Sculptor, died quite suddenly in a moment & poor Aunt Louise was *with him at the time*, when he was showing her some of his newest Busts – when he gave a shriek & fell forward & never spoke again – & she only heard a gurgling in his throat. She undid his collar, moved his arms, felt his pulse – but all in vain. She ran for help to his neighbour & pupil Mr Gilbert, & he sent for a Doctor & asked her to leave. Only the next Mng. did she know he was dead from heart & the bursting of a blood vessel. He was dead when she left. – It has been as you may *easily* imagine, a terrible shock to her, & she was dreadfully upset, for besides the horror of such a thing, he was a very kind friend of hers & she was his pupil. It is too terrible & *such* a loss. He is to be buried tomorrow at St Paul's, & she means to go. It was so sad yesterday at the Unveiling of that splendid statue of dear Uncle Fritz in St George's wh. he had just completed to feel that he was also gone.

I thought much of all of you Geschwister on the *14th & 15th* & of your poor Mother-in-law.          Ever your devoted Grandmama

V.R.I.

I have very happy letters from Moretta. I will send Ludwig's Card in a day or 2. Poor Sir E. Böhm must have had heart complaint for some time, but his death was caused by the bursting of the great artery near the heart.

[1] Princess Victoria of Prussia was sometimes called Vicky and at others Moretta to distinguish her from her mother, Vicky, Princess Royal and now Dowager German Empress, who called herself Empress Frederick.

Dec 29 1890

Darling Victoria,

In my last letter I said I must write to you about a *subject* wh. I had no time for, then. It is abt. Alicky & N. I had *your assurance* that *nothing was* to be *feared* in that quarter, but I *know* it *for certain*, that in spite of *all your* (Papa's Ernie's & your) *objections* & still more *contrary* to the *positive* wish of *his Parents* who do *not wish* him to *marry A.* as they feel, as everyone must do, for the *youngest* Sister to *marry* the *son of the Er.* [Emperor] – wld never answer, & lead to no happiness, – well in spite of all this behind *all* your backs, Ella & S. [Serge] do *all* they *can* to bring it *about*, encouraging & even urging the Boy to do it! – I promised *not* to mention who told *me* – I must do to you, it is *At Alix* who heard it from *At Minny*[1] *herself* who is very much annoyed abt. it. You must *never* mention *At. Alix's* name, but *this* must *not* be *allowed to go on*. Papa *must* put his foot down & there *must* be no more visits of Alicky to Russia – & *he must* & *you* & Ernie must insist on a *stop* being put to the whole affair.

The state of Russia is *so bad*, so rotten that at any moment something dreadful might happen & tho' it may not signify to Ella, the wife of the Thronfolger[2] is in a most difficult & precarious position.

I have written all to Papa, who *must* be *strong* & firm & I am so afraid he may *not* be. It wld have the very worst effect here & in Germany (where Russia is not liked) & wld. produce a gt separation between our families. Already Ernie & Alicky have not been here this year.

We continue to have bitterly cold weather. I am very anxious to hear how you think Moretta (Vicky) & Adolph are getting on & how you like the latter.

And now with renewed good wishes for the New Year in wh. we hope to meet ere long

Ever your devoted Grandmama

V.R.I.

I must thank you so very much for your dear letter of the 20th & the pretty card, dear little Alice's work. You must indeed miss Ludwig sadly.

[1] Princess Dagmar of Denmark, sister of Alexandra, Princess of Wales, and of King George I of the Hellenes. She married the Tsarevitch in 1866, when she became Marie Feodorovna, and became Empress when her husband succeeded his father in 1881. Minny, or Minnie, was rescued by the British Navy in the Black Sea after almost all the Romanoffs had been assassinated, and lived until 1928.

[2] Heir to the throne.

BALMORAL CASTLE

Sept 18 1891

Darling Victoria,

I wrote to dear Papa very soon after excellent Schoberth's[1] death (which is a great sorrow to us & a very great loss) asking if he cld. perhaps kindly recommend any one – some one like German, but he never answered. Then I wrote again for his birthday & said that I intended taking Harnak[1] [*sic*], Uncle Arthur's Valet (recommended to him by good Schoberth). But unfortunately he is not at all strong & is quite uncertain if he will be able to go on – I have taken him on trial for a year – & therefore I shld. be very glad if you & Papa cld. look out for someone to be in reserve.

You know how much dear Papa & I wish dear Alicky shld some day marry Max of Baden, whom I *formerly* wished for Maud[3] – but of late I have purposely not said any thing abt the *latter* as I am so anxious abt. the *former*. Now I hear he is at or is coming to Fredensborg & I am terribly afraid that some arrangement *might* be made – as the Gd. Parents & Uncle Bertie knew I was so anxious one of the cousins shld marry him. Then I heard that he did not at all wish to marry an English Prss: If (as I anticipate) nothing comes of this I hope dear Papa will *lose no time* in inviting him.

I had fondly hoped Ernie wld marry Maud but she is not very strong & he himself fear [*sic*] that, especially on account of the symptoms in dear Irène's beautiful boy[4] tho' these *I* think will get better, it wld not be advisable.

I hope & think all will be right about dear Ludwig's promotion.[5] Poor dear Auntie is well unberufen but it distresses me to see her carrying about this great burthen.[6] I trust *by very soon after* the 1st she will be freed from it.

---

[1] Charles Schoberth, Page of the Chamber to the Queen.

[2] J. H. F. Harnach, German valet to the Duke of Connaught.

[3] Princess Maud, daughter of the Prince and Princess of Wales. She married King Haakon VII of Norway.

[4] Two-year-old Prince Waldemar, who, in spite of haemophilia, lived until he was fifty-six.

[5] He was promoted Captain on 30 December 1891 at the unusually early age of thirty-eight.

[6] Princess Beatrice's boy, Prince Maurice of Battenberg, was born at Balmoral 3 October 1891. He was killed during the retreat from Mons in 1914 while serving in the British Army.

Give my affte love to your dear Mother in Law & Franzjos if he is
still with you & a kiss to the little ones.

Ever your devoted Mama [*sic*]
V.R.I.

Do send me a good new Photograph of the Baby & also of little Louise.


BALMORAL CASTLE
Sept 30 1891

Darling Victoria,

I hope that you may perhaps be able to tell us the real facts concerning
poor dear little Alix, illness & death.[1] We know really nothing
except this telegram & dear Ella sent more extraordinary explanations
by telegram but has never *once written*. 1st. What brought on the fits?
As a usual thing – a wrong state of the kidneys produces these con-
vulsions if *not* attended to; & the labour must then be brought on (wh.
is *quite* easily done) but the danger is very great. Now, as she had been
very ill in her 1st confinement, and was very anaemic, her blood was
probably in a bad state & the heart weak (wh. darling Ella called in a
telegram 'flatulency' of the heart) she cld not bear any shock & the dis-
order of the kidneys produced blood poisoning. Do try & tell me the
truth, wh. we are painfully anxious to know. Perhaps you cld get the
aertzliche Bericht[2] from Ella. It is too terribly sad, & so awful for poor
Ella happening on a visit to her. The poor little children, I do hope Ella
will have charge of them.

Our letters crossed. Let me thank you now for your last dear one of
the 18th.

I hope all will be right about Louis' promotion in the winter.

Dear Auntie is unberufen quite wonderfully well & active doing
everything, but since Sunday it may be any day & we *hope* this week.

I only hope Ernie won't arrive the *very* day! But we shall be so pleased
to see him! It is 3 or 4 years since he was here!

Ever your devoted Mama [*sic*]
V.R.I.

Pray answer this soon.

Today is poor Empress Augusta's birthday. I hope Irène's & Henry's
visit to Baden went off well. It turned out Max of Baden's visit to
Copenhagen was only for 2 days & before Maud arrived!

[1] This Alix is Princess Alexandra of Greece, sister of Victoria's son-in law
Andrew, who married Grand Duke Paul of Russia, Ella's brother-in-law.
She died in childbirth while staying with Ella and Serge.

[2] Medical report.

BALMORAL CASTLE

Oct 22 1891

Darling Victoria,

I have to thank you for 2 dear letters of the 2nd & 3rd & write to say that I entirely approve what you say abt. Alicky & Max of Baden. It would be much better if Alicky had *at least* another year to gain in strength & health. So much depends on *that*, & from what Aunt Marie wrote to me I fear this was gtly. neglected in poor little Alix's case. The Doctors say she was in such a bad state of health that she wld probably not have lived long. The kidneys quite wrong & the heart very weak & she was very ill already the 1st time & I believe her health was not properly attended to *before* her marriage.

Thank God! dear Auntie seems to get better & stronger each time, tho' I hope she will stop now for many reasons – She is moving abt. now & has sat up since Saturday. She never has had a single drawback. The Baby (who ought to have been a girl) is a big fine strong Child & dark.

So many thanks for the Photographs of your lovely little girls & your dear self. Little Louise is just like what little Alice *was* – Dear Ernie looks very well & is in high spirits, but he has a cough & says he has had it so long. He ought not to go to Potsdam but to you to Malta.

I hope you will tell Papa that if this cough continues or gets worse from fresh cold – that he must leave Potsdam at once & go south. He is too precious to risk anything, & it is too dangerous.

Victoria & Ernie are very funny together.[1] I am sure they have written & told you every thing. We have had some dancing – Later on I think there will be a little play.

And now with every wish for a good & prosperous journey & passage

Ever your devoted Mama [*sic*]

V.R.I.

Although the Queen had at first judged as unsuitable a match between her grandson and heir to the throne (after his father the Prince of Wales) and Princess May of Teck, she was entirely won round and was delighted at the idea of Eddy, Prince Albert Victor, Duke of Clarence, becoming engaged to the Princess in December 1891. Besides, she had by this time become reconciled

[1] Princess Victoria Melita, the Edinburghs' lively daughter, had much in common with the future Grand Duke. The Queen always hoped that they would marry.

to the fact that Alicky of Hesse would never change her mind about her English cousin.

By an extraordinary stroke of fate, the twenty-seven-year-old Prince, whose health had never been robust, died almost immediately after the announcement of the engagement. The Queen, stunned with grief, noted with dark satisfaction that her grandson had conformed to Royal tradition by dying on 'the *14th*'.

A second, but less unexpected misfortune occurred two months later (missing the 14th by only one day) in the death of the Grand Duke of Hesse. Ernie succeeded his father as Grand Duke Ernst-Ludwig.

OSBORNE

Feb 3 1892

Darling Victoria,

These lines will reach you at Darmstadt where dear Papa will be delighted to see you & Alicky too.

I have to thank you for three dear letters of 28th Dec with dear little Alice's letter, of the 10th & 15th. Jany.

This last so very dear, kind one was written on hearing of the *terrible* calamity wh. has befallen us all as well as the Country. The feeling of grief & sympathy is universal & great. Was there ever anything so sad, so tragic?

It is really an overwhelming misfortune, & I believe Auntie has written you some of the sad, sad details! The real & actual illness only lasted from the Saturday 9th to the *14th* (that fatal date) – & the last 48 hours had flown to the brain & caused fearful delirium.

It was evident that there was blood poisoning for Dr Broadbent the clever Dr. who, with Dr Laking attended Georgie[1] as well as him, said that he died from the effects of it – just as if he had taken a dose of Prussic Acid. When you think that his poor young Bride who had come to spend his birthday with him, came to see him die – it is one of the most fearful tragedies one can imagine. It wld. sound unnatural & overdrawn if it was put into a Novel.

Uncle Bertie, Aunt Alix, Georgie & the girls came here yesterday, & I hope will be the better for the change. Uncle B.[2] looks very pale & sad & aged, but is not ill; Aunt Alix is grown very thin & looks so sad & delicate. It is too sad to see her so. Georgie is thin, his hair cut quite short & the merriment gone out of him at present.[3] But he does not

---

[1] Prince George, Eddy's younger brother, and now heir to the throne after his father. He had had typhoid fever.

[2] Uncle Bertie, the heartbroken Prince of Wales.

[3] Prince George was devoted to his elder brother.

look ill. The shock to his nerves however has been very great. The universal sympathy is quite marvellous & touching & even abroad.

I fear you will find it very cold after Malta & trust it will do the children no harm. It is a bad time of year to return *from* the south. – You will I trust find dear Papa much better. It was a great disappointment not to see him here for that sad occasion.

I am so glad you liked Alice's Picture as I thought it lovely & so like.

Many thanks also for the pretty glass lamps you gave me for Christmas.

We are so looking forward to seeing you in the course of this month, but you will find us very dull I fear – as of course – our deep mourning prevents anything being done.

With kind love to Ludwig,

Ever your devoted Grandmama<br>V.R.I.

I hope you found your dear Mother-in-Law well. I send you a photograph of the Albert Chapel as it was on the day of the funeral. Poor darling Eddy, he was so good & gentle, & I shall miss him greatly. In the photograph of the Albert Chapel you will see that dear Eddy rests between dear Grandpapa's Cenotaph & dear Uncle Leop<sup>d</sup>'s tomb, & there he is ultimately to be placed.

WINDSOR CASTLE

March 6 1892

Darling Victoria,

You may imagine my distress & anxiety at these most distressing news! Darling Papa, you know *how* I love him & how the thought of this terrible attack alarms and distresses me – for him & for you beloved Children! I wld. like to go at once to you – but will not do what wld alarm & agitate him, however, I will try & go & see you on my way back as I shld not be happy unless I had seen him.

What cld have caused this? Do write *every day*, one of you, You, or Irène or Alicky or Ludwig & I *must* have a daily telegram from Dr Eichenbrod who has just now telegraphed an answer to my enquiry. It sounds serious – but please God! he will recover the use of that side gradually. I long for details. Is Ella coming? Are you in the House?

I can think of nothing else. We seem to be doomed to trouble sorrow & sickness! It is terrible!

God help us all & bless you my own darlings.

Ever your devoted & very much distressed<br>Grandmama<br>V.R.I.

WINDSOR CASTLE

March 15 1892

Poor darling Victoria,

This is *too terrible*! What *must your* grief be, you who were so devoted to that beloved Father, who was Father & Mother to you, to help & serve whom – your life has been so devoted! It adds to *my quite overwhelming* grief to think of your distress & of poor dear Ernie & Alicky alone – *Orphans*!! It is *awful*. But I am *still there* & while I live Alicky, till she is married, will be *more* than *ever my own Child* – as you *all* are. Wilhelmine has kindly written all details of the last day – & hours – wh. are heartrending to read.

Can poor dear little Alice take it in at all? I trust she will never forget her dear GdPapa.

What an *inexpressible* blessing & comfort it is that He knew you all & was so pleased to see you. – How different to poor dear Mama – who had neither her Husband or one Child near her & died so full of grief for little May & full of anxiety for the others!

I cannot write more today.

Ever your most devoted Grandmama

V.R.I.

I feel much for Ludwig who hurried back to this dreadful Scene. Tenderest love to sisters whom I will write to as soon as I can.

Thousands of thanks for your dear letters wh. were such a comfort as they told me all.

WINDSOR CASTLE

May 18 1892

Darling Victoria,

Your dear letter of the 12th gave me great pleasure tho' it is very sad & so it must always be now. I *can't* realise the dreadful truth! He was so dear & joyous – so loving & so young of [*sic*] his age – that the blank must be terrible & for poor Alicky above all, – tho' you were the one He confided in most.

After a very hot week, since Sunday it has been colder & windier again.

When Sir Wm. Jenner was here I spoke to him abt. the possibility of Ernie's marrying one of the Edinburgh Cousins,[1] & he said there was no danger & no objection as they are so strong & healthy & Aunt

[1] The Queen was now pressing Ernie, the Grand Duke of Hesse, to marry his cousin Princess Victoria Melita ('Ducky'). The scourge of haemophilia was by now strongly in the Queen's mind, but she gladly accepted Sir William Jenner's contention that first-cousin marriages were strengthening.

Marie also. He said if the relations were strong intermarriage with them only led to g^ter strength & health.

I have written this to Ernie himself & I hope you will also tell him, – & Eigenbrodt & Orchie especially who is very foolish abt. it.

I am glad to hear you are feeling better. I hope to settle abt. a Doctor for you. With love to Ludwig & kisses to the Darlings

Ever your devoted Grandmama

V.R.I.

BALMORAL CASTLE

June 2 1892

Darling Victoria,

I send you my present for dear Alicky's birthday & will write to her tomorrow. It is an Enamel of your darling Papa whom I think of so often. Many loving thanks for your dear letter of the 21st, & charming present for my old birthday wh. made me also very sad as darling Papa had begun giving them to me. And Oh! when I think of last year when He & your 2 sisters were with me & we all so happy together, I *can't believe that that* is past for *ever* in *this* World! It is *too terrible*. How you & dear Alicky must miss him! – I hope Alicky will show you the letter I wrote abt. Ernie – & At. H. & T? [Helena and her elder daughter 'Thora' (Princess Helena Victoria).] I trust Ernie & Alicky will be *here then*.

We have been much startled lately to hear of *Missy's*[1] *Engagement* to *Ferdinand of Rumania*. He is nice I believe & the Parents are charming – but the Country is very insecure & the immorality of the Society at Bucharest *quite awful*. Of course the marriage would be delayed some time as Missy won't be 17 till the end of Oct:! – I hope Ernie will have shewn you what I wrote him abt. what Sir Wm. Jenner said relative to Ducky? I forgot I wrote it to you. –

We have had warm & again very fine weather on the whole since the 1st two or 3 days but a gt. deal of rain lately – tho' chiefly at night. Today was wet till about 5.

Thank Ludwig for his 2 letters wh. I shall hope soon to answer.

I shall be able to get a safe & good Dr. for you who can come sooner & remain longer. *When* is it[2] to be?

Ever your devoted Grandmama

V.R.I.

[1] Marie, Princess of Edinburgh, who married Ferdinand, Crown Prince of Rumania in 1893.

[2] Victoria was expecting another child, Prince George of Battenberg (1892–1938), later the second Marquess of Milford Haven.

The people here are so grieved abt. dear Papa, & I think & talk of him so often.

OSBORNE

Aug 4 1892

Darling Victoria,

I was going to write & thank you for your dear letter of the 26th when this dreadful fire[1] took place & I had so much to write, besides William's[2] visit (tho' I saw very little of him) & the worries of a change of Gov*t*[3] impending and visitors etc to see that I cld not manage to write sooner.

It is too terrible & so distressing for poor Auntie that it shld have happened in her room! The terror she was in lest you shd. suffer from this fright – Ludwig being away besides. How störend[4] in the pleasant stay with you & your Mother-in-Law. Really too distressing. The loss of Auntie's pearls is a real sorrow to me – but all *that*, is nothing in comparison to what *might* have been & we must thank God! that you are all safe!

Ludwig is sailing abt. but we managed to let him hear. It must have given him a gt. shock as it did me!

I hope you are really feeling quite right again? *Comfortable* one *cannot* feel in your condition. It is a gt. relief that Dr Champneys is going to you.

I must end, Ever your devoted Grandmama

V.R.I.

On 22 June 1893, in the course of manoeuvres off Syria in the eastern Mediterranean, the flagship of the Royal Navy's Mediterranean Fleet, H.M.S. *Victoria*, was rammed by the flagship of the fleet's second division, H.M.S. *Camperdown*. The *Victoria* filled and sank rapidly in a flat calm, taking down 358 of her company, including the peppery Commander-in-Chief, Admiral Sir George Tryon. The disaster was a great personal blow to the Queen and

---

[1] At Heiligenberg. Princess Beatrice was the guest of her mother-in-law at the time.

[2] Wilhelm. The Kaiser, a keen yachtsman, had come over from Germany for Cowes week.

[3] The Liberals were back in power with a majority of forty.

[4] Disturbing.

a notable *cause célèbre*. The Earl of Clanwilliam was an Admiral and C.-in-C. Portsmouth; his son, Lieutenant Lord Gillford, was Tryon's Flag Lieutenant who risked his career in trying to prevent the tragedy.

OSBORNE

July 22 1893

Darling Victoria,

So many thanks for your dear letter. I am so thankful to have been able to be of use to you & the darling Children & that this disagreeable but (as it proves) necessary operation has been so successfully carried out. Have the children been able to get a little fresh air or must they not go out?

I must tell you *how* I enjoyed those 10 quiet days with your beloved ones! I don't know when I felt happier during the last few years. You are all just like my own Children & in one of dear Mama's letters to me, she recommended *you* most specially to me in case of any thing happening to her. Poor little Leopold[1] has again hurt his ankle just after you left & is being carried again! You will be sorry to hear that poor Franz Teck has lost his youngest (Married) Sister.[2] Bss or Gräfin Hügel who died at Gratz 2 days ago in consequence of an operation.

We expect George & May here on the 31st. Thora[3] comes on the 29th with her Father.

I saw Ld. Clanwilliam yesterday who was very much affected in speaking of the 'Victoria', & of the gt. pain it was to his son having to say what he did. He & all say poor Sir G. Tryon was such a loss. I had a most touching letter from poor Lady Tryon who feels her loss very deeply & is much upset by the C. Martial. She had just got back his *Cap* wh. must have been dreadful but is a gt. comfort to her to have. – They have had so much rain here that it is greener than I remember it for long & looks lovely & fresh.

With many kisses to the dear Children

Ever your devoted Grandmama

V.R.I.

I am very glad you have been sitting to Tuxen & that the picture promises so well.

[1] Prince Leopold of Battenberg, Princess Beatrice's second son, a haemophiliac.

[2] Amelia, Princess of Teck, Countess von Hügel.

[3] Princess Helena Victoria of Schleswig-Holstein.

BALMORAL CASTLE

Sept 24 1893

Darling Victoria,

I have been a terrible time without writing to you, & I hope you will excuse me, but I have had so much to write lately on business that I cld. not attend to my dearest corresponders. Besides I must spare my eyes at night so am desired not to write late at night & this takes away from the time when I used to write.

Many thanks for your dear letter of the 30th ult. after poor dear Uncle Ernest's[1] death. It was a gt. shock reminding of past happy days many years ago when poor dear Uncle used to come & see us so often & was very kind to me & also very kind to all our Children – & I cannot forget that he was darling Grandpapa's *only* Brother.

25th – I cld. not finish yesterday, so I go on today. Of course my interest in dear old Coburg is *very great now* that Uncle Affie is Duke.[2] If this were to happen it cld. not do so at a better time for his active Naval career was, as you may say finished & we did not know what occupation he wld. have, & *now* he has a gt. deal to do & seems most anxious to do it well. – He has set abt. everything wisely.

I hope & trust that the sad disagreement abt. the Rolfs[3] will come to an end, & that they will no longer be a cause of dispute & dispeace – as *both* are pensioned.

I had it out with Aunt Marie having written kindly but strongly to her. She is most anxious abt. Ernie & Ducky & I have written *twice* to Ernie abt. the *necessity* of his showing some attention & interest. Pray tell it him & say he *must answer* me. – Aunt Marie fears *he* no longer wishes it, wh. I am sure is not the case. Georgie lost Missy by waiting & waiting.

Mary Adams gets on very well & I hope feels comfortable.

We shall have the gt happiness of seeing darling Ella with Serge & Paul here on Thursday. Such a pleasure to see dear Ella again.

Georgie & May[4] have been staying at Osborne for a fortnight & again here for a fortnight with us & I can't tell you *how* much we all like her. She is so amiable, sensible & rightminded. I think we are very fortunate in getting such a wife for Georgie & they seem quite happy

---

[1] Ernest II of Saxe-Coburg-Gotha, Prince Albert's elder brother.

[2] The Duke of Edinburgh had succeeded as Duke of Saxe-Coburg-Gotha.

[3] Dr Rolf, tutor to Prince Alfred of Edinburgh.

[4] Princess May of Teck, soon after the death of Eddy, became engaged to his younger brother instead. She became Queen Mary in 1910 and died 24 March 1953.

& contented together & he is very dear & affte. & also very right-minded & steady.

This letter will just reach you before you leave. – Hoping soon to hear from you.

Ever your devoted Grandmama
V.R.I.

Love to Ludwig. Aunt Marie is at Sinaia & in abt. a fortnight or 3 weeks we may expect Missy's[1] confinement.

1894 was another eventful year for the Queen, full of sadnesses alleviated by several joys. The accident referred to in the first letter occurred to the seven-year-old Princess Victoria Eugénie, Princess Beatrice's daughter, who had been tossed and rolled on by her pony. Brain damage was at first suspected, but all was well, and she grew up a lovely fair-haired Princess who took on the lively and hazardous duty of being Queen of Spain.

The worry caused by this mishap was offset by the marriage, at last, of Ernie, Grand Duke of Hesse to Princess Victoria Melita, Ducky. It was a union the Queen had long hoped for and con-spired to bring about, but which the highly-strung, artistic Ernie had entered into only after the gravest heart-searchings.

Then, at Richmond Park on 23 June, the Duchess of York (May of Teck) gave birth to a boy, the future King Edward VIII and Duke of Windsor, ensuring the succession through no fewer than three further generations.

Against these happy events had to be set the tragedy of lovely Alicky. Early in the year, the Queen was full of hope that the affair between Princess Alix and the Tsarevitch was, after all, at an end. But at the Hessian wedding she heard that they had in fact become formally engaged, and that she had lost her last Hessian grand-daughter to 'horrid Russia'. (She also knew that, as well as Ella, Willy, the German Emperor, had been a party to the conspiracy to bring about this union.)

In June the Tsarevitch arrived in England to enjoy the delight of seeing his fiancée again ('who looked lovely and more beautiful than ever', he told his mother) and to endure the ordeal of a close and critical examination by Queen Victoria at Windsor Castle.

---

[1] The Queen of Rumania, the Queen's grand-daughter Marie, had given birth to a son, the future King Carol II, on 16 October 1893.

Tragic events in Russia hastened Alicky's and Nicky's wedding. The health of the Tsar, a giant of a man not yet fifty years old, rapidly deteriorated through the year, and he died on 1 November.

Nicky was now Emperor of All the Russias, and it was considered appropriate for the young couple to marry immediately after the funeral.

For the Queen, a more direct and personal anxiety was the ill-health of her Private Secretary, Sir Henry Ponsonby. The prospect of facing the new year without his kind and tactful guidance, and the intimate relationship built up over the years, was hard to bear.

OSBORNE

Feb 15 1894

Darling Victoria,

All our plans have had to be changed on acct. of poor darling Ena's dreadful fall (wh. at 1st seemed nothing) – tho' thank God! she is out of danger today tho' still the g$^{test}$ care is necessary in case of any possible (tho' unlikely) complication and we cannot well leave for Windsor till this day week. I wish therefore to know if Ernie & Alicky wld. not like to come here or else we shall *not* have the *pleasure* of seeing them for 3 *weeks* even? & *may* I keep the Children till Tuesday 19th [20th].

Please telegraph the answer early to these 2 questions.

We have gone thro' terrible anxiety since Saturday evg. tho' she *began* to get a *little better* that very night & she has gone *on steadily* improving ever since. I fear *she* cannot be moved next week. –

Be sure & telegraph soon tomorrow. – I *long* to see Ernie & Alicky! –

Ever your devoted Grandmama

V.R.I.

I wonder if poor dear Alicky has talked to you abt. the *end* of Niki's hopes. At Alix & Victoria say he is miserable & that our dear Ella *always* encouraged him instead of doing the reverse.

VILLA FABBRICOTTI, FLORENCE

Ap 3 1894

Darling Victoria,

Accept my very warmest good wishes for your dear birthday wh. I trust you will spend happily at Walton.[1] My present to you & Ludwig

---

[1] Louis and Victoria had rented a house by the river at Walton-on-Thames. It was the scene of the happy reunion between Nicky and Alicky.

for your 2 birthdays is a copy of the head of dear Sandro's Picture wh. I have got. – I shall think so much of him on that day –

I am writing in the garden & since a few days it is quite warm. The 1st ten or 12 days commencing from 2 days after we came it was very cold, that is the wind was very cold tho' the sun was (except 3 days) very bright. But not a drop of rain wh. has retarded the vegetation much.

Pray thank dear little Alice for her beautifully written letter.

My tiresome arms & legs cause such trouble in getting in & out of the Carriage that I have only been to one Gallery of Pictures (the Pitti).

I must end now rejoicing to meet you at Coburg for the great Event of darling Ernie's Wedding. Love to Ludwig.

Ever your devoted Grandmama<br>V.R.I.

A kiss to my precious little ones.

BALMORAL CASTLE

May 25 1894

Darling Victoria,

*How* can I thank you enough for your *charming* present, so wonderfully well painted & so prettily illustrated, I could not believe you had done it yourselves. It is such a delightful idea. I will keep it for very particularly pretty photographs of the family, grownups & Children.

We had a lovely warm day yesterday & went some way to take our tea out & in the evng we had some very pretty Tableaux wh. Mr Yorke[1] arranged.

Respecting Alicky & Uncle Bertie & Aunt Alix being hurt – it is quite absurd – I only asked to keep her as she was *not* going with me to Scotland, wh. Aunt Alix was *not* aware of & she quite understood me when I explained to her.

If any one *has* a right to be *offended* it is *I* – who am *never allowed* to have Victoria & Maud[2] to visit me, when *all* my *other* Grand Children come & stay with me. I call it unkind & especially very selfish; but that is *not Uncle's* fault.

You may say what I say, but I wld. not have objected to 2 nights at Sandringham only it was cruel to wish to take her away from me who knows best & am losing so much of her. Marlborough House[3] I do *not*

---

[1] Hon. Alexander Yorke, Groom-in-Waiting.

[2] The daughters of the Prince and Princess of Wales.

[3] The London home of the Prince and Princess of Wales. In the eyes of some people (including the Queen) its somewhat raffish reputation had not diminished with the passage of time.

wish for more than *a night*, or *outside* 2 nights & I don't wish her to go to Clarence Hse.[1] either. If she *can* interrupt her cure[2] & if she is *only* taken to the Opera or play – & *not* to *gt. dinners* or functions I, of course, *cld. not* object. She must *not* go to the State Balls or concerts unless Niky is there & wishes it. – For her dear birthday, she must *not* be left quite alone & you really must go & spend it with her. It is probably her *last* unmarried birthday & she really *must* not be left alone. Do promise that you will go to her.

Today is Aunt Lenchen's[3] birthday. Louie[4] has arrived & she thinks her looking well.

Oh! darling Victoria, the more I think of sweet Alicky's marriage the more unhappy I am! *Not* as to the personality, for I like him *very much* but on acct. of the Country the policy & differences with us & the awful insecurity to wh. that sweet Child will be exposed. To think she is learning Russian & will have probably to talk to a Priest – my whole nature rises up agst it – in spite of my efforts to be satisfied. –

But I will *try* & bear it & make the best of it. Still the feeling that I had laboured so hard to *prevent it* & that I felt at last there was *no longer* any danger & all in one night – *everything* was changed. Ella shld never have encouraged it originally as she did – at one time.

I must end with renewed thanks for your charming present, & believe me always,

Your devoted Grandmama<br>V.R.I.

Let Ludwig see this letter.

OSBORNE
Aug 21 1894

Darling Victoria,

So many thanks for your dear letter of the 6th giving the very touching account of the removal of the dear Remains of your beloved Father-in-law & of the ceremony at the Heiligenberg wh. must have been very trying to your dear Mother-in-law & so sad that *one* of her dear Children was missing! But it must be a great comfort to her to have it so close by & to be able to go there at all times.

We were much distressed to hear that Ludwig had been so unwell but I hope he is quite well again. He was I think a little overworked & that caused the throat to get so bad.

[1] The London home of the Duke and Duchess of Saxe-Coburg-Gotha.

[2] Princess Alix suffered from sciatica and took the cure at Harrogate, all German cures having failed.

[3] Princess Helena.

[4] Princess Helena's daughter, Princess Marie Louise.

The Photogravure has succeeded beautifully & I am sending 2 impresses asking to have one back & also a signature of Ludwig with the date. I pay for the Plate & you can then order as many Impresses as you like. – I enclose the direction. – I think you will all be pleased with it.

22nd. I could not finish last night so I do (now). I am anxious that you shld. see my letter to Ernie abt. Ducky whose expectations are a gt. joy & what I say abt. a good Dr. You must strongly impress this upon him, for her life & the Child's[1] may depend on it, & your experience can prove that. I am rather anxious to know abt. when the Event is likely to take place on acct. of *my plans*.

At last I had a long letter from Ella yesterday. I must end now & hope the dear Children are well.

Ever your devoted Grandmama<br>V.R.I.

BALMORAL CASTLE

Sept 6 1894

Darling Victoria,

I meant to answer you before your last dear letter of the 27th before this, but we were in the midst of our packing – & then came the dreadful news of dear good Sir J. Cowell's[2] death wh. upset me very much & wh. I am sure has grieved you all very much.

I send you an acct. of the sad event written by Ld. E. Clinton[3] who went there at once. The regret is universal. He was so much respected & liked & was such a good man, so truly religious & always prepared to go! It was a beautiful painless, peaceful end, no suffering, no pain of parting, but dreadful for her! I add a copy of a letter from Ad. Fullerton wh. I thought Ludwig wld. like to read. Please send them on to At. Lenchen after Ernie Ducky & Alicky have seen them asking Auntie to return them.

I come now to the part of your letter concerning the Dr & Nurse for Ducky. As regards the latter I quite agree that if At. Marie for this 1st time wishes to have this Russian Nurse one must not make objections. And as regards the Dr. I also *quite* understand the necessity for Ernie not to offend German prejudice, but on the other hand I *know* that *similar* ideas were the *cause* of an incompetent Dr being the *cause* of

---

[1] The Grand Duchess of Hesse ('Ducky') was with child. Princess Elizabeth of Hesse was born 11 March 1895 and died at the age of eight.

[2] Master of the Household.

[3] Groom-in-Waiting who succeeded Sir John Cowell.

*William's Arm*, & a *lifelong* injury & blemish[1] – & you know that Dr [illegible] at Darmstadt treated you & another one poor Marie Erbach & this *outweighs any other consideration*. Dr Champneys having attended you twice it wld come very naturally. While *German Oculists* & *even Surgeons* are *cleverer* than *ours*, – there is *not* a doubt that in the particular line of *childbirth* & *women's* illnesses the English are the *best* in the World, more skilful & *much* more *delicate*. Aunt Marie does not *know* this, as she never had *but* one English Doctor. –

It is essential for me to know soon abt. it & when it is to be.

7th. – I finish today. The Bazar [*sic*] was an immense success & so pretty & amusing. They realized £2399. I send newspaper accts. to Alicky.

We have deplorable weather – such rain & very little sun.

The poor Comte de Paris[2] is quite dying.

Ever your devoted Grandmama<br>
V.R.I.

I will send Ad. Fullerton's letter tomorrow.


When it became clear that the Tsar was dying, Nicky telegraphed from his father's bedside to Alicky at Darmstadt to join him. Victoria accompanied her young sister until Ella could take over the escort duty.

BALMORAL CASTLE

Oct 21 1894

Darling Victoria,

'L'homme propose & Dieu dispose'! Never was saying true [*sic*] than this at the present moment when you 4 sisters hoped to be quietly & happily together & now two of you have had to leave on such a sad errand. If only the long journey & great gemüths bewegung[3] do not hurt poor darling Alicky, who already has had so much to go through & it will be so trying besides the fatigue. It makes me very anxious & unhappy! All my fears abt. her future marriage now show themselves so strongly & my blood runs cold when I think of her *so* young most likely placed on that vy. unsafe Throne, her dear life & above all her Husband's constantly threatened & unable to see her but rarely; It is a great additional anxiety in my declining years! Oh! how I wish it was not to be that I shld lose my sweet Alicky. All I *most earnestly* ask now is

---

[1] The Emperor's birth had been a breech delivery which the Queen ascribed to German gynaecological incompetence. Willy's withered arm, second only to haemophilia, became the most notable and influential royal disability in modern history.

[2] Louis Philippe, grandson of King Louis Philippe, died 8 September 1894.

[3] Emotional stress.

that *nothing* shld be *settled* for her *future without* my *being told* before. She has *no Parents* & I am her only *Grandparent* & feel *I have* a *claim* on her! She is like my *own Child* as you *all* are my dear Children but she & he are orphans. Ernie to whom I telegraphed this said, there was *no* question of anything requiring his presence but he seems very low. It must have been terrible for him to see her go!

Do explain what I have said to Nicky & also to both that I *do* pray that (at any time) she will come to see me once more before she marries. Do, do that. I feel as if she was being carried off already.

I am grieved that you are already going off from England by P. & O of the 15th Nov. as I am so afraid we shall miss you. If only it had been on the 22nd. –

I am very glad [word missing] is gone also with her & do tell Gretchen & Frn: Schneider[1] to write every 2 or 3 days as Alicky may not have time to write often & I am *so anxious* to be kept au fait of what is going on.

Now goodbye & God bless you & I can think of nothing else.

Liko has just returned & says Ludwig's Ship[2] is splendid.

Ever your devoted Grandmama

V.R.I.

This illness of the poor Emperor is too, too sad – & has come so suddenly – but I hear Professor Leydon thinks it has existed some time & *before* the Influenza. I feel so much for poor At. Minnie.

BALMORAL CASTLE

Nov 7 1894

Darling Victoria,

Tho' I shall D.V. see you so soon, I must write to thank you for your dear dear & sensible letter of the 5th recd. today explaining the reason for dear Alicky's serious decision to have her Wedding so soon & Ernie's for agreeing to it.

When I heard it by telegraph (I think on Sunday) it gave me a dreadful shock for tho' I dreaded it wld be so I hoped agst. hope. I cannot deny that it is *impossible* it should be *otherwise* – & that it is best for darling Alicky – she wld fret & worry away from Nicky – & her position at home or with us be very difficult. And lastly it is a gt. advantage for her that she shld begin her life there quite quietly & the wedding be very quiet. – Still the disappointment of not seeing her again as my *sweet* innocent *gentle* Alicky is *very very great* – for alas I am sure it will be then as a *mighty Empress*!!

[1] Alicky's Russian tutor.
[2] The cruiser H.M.S. *Cambrian*.

And *cela me revolte* to feel she has been taken *possession* of & carried away as it were by these Russians. I wish she had *not* gone to Livadia & *yet* that was also impossible!

By your telegram I know you are not going to Petersburg & that Irène stops with poor Ducky.

I am so distressed abour poor Miss Robson. *What* are you to do if she can't leave her Mother? You must get *somebody* temporarily.

In haste Ever your devoted Grandmama

V.R.I.

I am *so* longing to see you. I *wld* have got Auntie B. to go to Alicky's Wedding to represent me but I fear now there is no longer time.

Let me again thank you for your dear firm letter explaining Alicky's departure & decision to conform at once to the Greek religion: dated Oct. 23.

BUCKINGHAM PALACE

Feb 19 1895

Darling Victoria,

I have not thanked you for your last dear letters of Nov. 10 & 26 Dec. by which I am so glad to hear that you are all well. I am looking so very much forward to seeing Ludwig whose letters I am so sorry not to have answered, but there has been no time. There has been so much to do lately. – We came here yesterday direct from Osborne with Aunt Vicky – but were obliged to leave Liko behind with a bad attack of lumbago – wh. came on 3 or 4 days after he hurt, & indeed put out, his shoulder on the ice on the 11th – We hope he will rejoin us at Windsor tomorrow – Alas! poor Sir Henry Ponsonby is in a very sad state, his poor mind not being recovered, tho' his arm & leg have to a great extent done so. The future is very sad & dark I fear – & it is quite terrible for poor Lady Ponsonby & poor Maggie & also the sons.

We have had exceptionally cold weather at Osborne ever since the 2nd of Jany. with the exception of a few days in the middle of the month – Frost every night & several times 16 17 even! Some snow, but above all such a piercing cold N.E. wind.

Ducky is I hear expecting the event[1] in 3 weeks time. At Marie wld. not have Dr Champneys & began saying she ought to have a German Dr, or else Dr Playfair – so I said I withdrew fr my offer & hoped she wld get a good *German*, wh. I thought from Ernie's letter *was* going to be when I got a letter from At Minnie saying Dr *Playfair* was ready to come for a moderate fee.

*I* had a gt. deal of trouble abt. him last year & so I have left it for At.

[1] The birth of Princess Elizabeth of Hesse.

Marie to settle & shall have nothing to do with it! Dr Playfair is very unvorträglich[1] & the very reverse of Dr Champneys tho' he is a clever Dr. – I hope & trust all will go well –

It is much milder today – I regret Nicky's speech the other day wh is *contrary* to the way he began.

I am sending Alice a birthday present wh. [I] hope you will like & intend to give all my Gt gd daughters one like it.

Ever your devoted Grandmama<br>V.R.I.

Love to Ludwig & kisses to the [word indecipherable but probably children.]

GRAND HOTEL CIMIEZ, NICE

March 31 1895

Darling Victoria,

Let me now wish you many many happy returns of your dear birthday & every blessing that God can bestow in this – alas! so [un]certain World. My present goes to Darmstadt – but Ludwig will bring you a trifle from here.

We have excellent fine & except the two days brilliantly bright weather, – only the last 4 or 5 rather gusty weather with a good deal of wind. It is a gt pleasure to see Ludwig here, & he is immensely admired. He will tell you all abt our days here. Eugè Leuchtenberg[2] & her Brother Youri[3] & his handsome nice wife[4] we have seen several times They have most lovely Children.

Aunt Alexandrine we have seen already 5 times & she is looking very well. Also Aunt Clem[5] & Philippe She looks well but is quite broken & crushed by the loss of dear Amélie.[6]

This very early Christening at Darmstadt is very unusual. But Ernie made some explanation of its being to prevent having a number of people wh. otherwise wld. have been necessary and wh. wld have been too fatiguing for her. It seems that Baby is very like what your

---

[1] Not very presentable.

[2] Eugénie, the Duchess of Leuchtenberg (1845–1925).

[3] Or 'Yuri', Russian for George, Prince Romanovsky, 5th Duke of Leuchtenberg.

[4] Anastasia, Princess of Montenegro. Yuri's second wife.

[5] Princess Clémentine, widow of Prince Augustus of Saxe-Coburg-Gotha and Prince Albert's cousin. She was also the daughter of Louis Philippe, King of France. Philippe was her eldest son.

[6] Daughter to above.

Sisters & Ernie were. I wld have preferred its being called Alice, but Eliz^th is very appropriate.

I *do* wish you *cld* get Ernie to be less neglectful in answering letters & telegrams. He never thanked the Dss. of Roxburghe for her Wedding present; he has never answered At Vicky's letter of congratulation on the little girl's birth; he has never answered Aunty B's telegram of congratulation – in short he is neglectful even to me I have to send message on message by telegram. He will become very unpopular & already there are gt. complaints. He also devotes too much time on [illegible word] & neglects the Army. Do, I entreat you do what you can to make him more punctual & more attentive.[1]

2nd Ap: Yesterday poor dear Sandro's widow[2] came to see me. Ludwig brought her; & I was so pleased with & touched by her. She is so handsome, so pleasing & so very distinguée. But she looks so sad. She was very much upset at seeing me. Auntie Beatrice is equally pleased with her & she had been to visit her at Menton.

Eugénie Oldenburg & Youry Leuchtenberg & his handsome & very pleasing wife are here. Her sister Pss. Militza of Montenegro, is also here at Beaulieu & comes over with her Husband the Gd. Duke Peter. Eugenie is charming.

I heard yesterday from Alicky who seems very happy at Tsarskoe Selo where however they still have snow! Ludwig will take this letter also. We have really splendid weather ever since we came. I am writing in the garden where we also breakfasted today. Tonight we are going to hear the splendid Russian singers whom you & we admired so much at Darmstadt and Windsor led by Slawianski d'agruna, a gt treat.

I must thank you now for your last dear letter of the 14th March.

Kissing the dear Children, Ever your devoted Grandmama

V.R.I.

BALMORAL CASTLE

Sept 19 1895

Darling Victoria,

I was just going to write & thank you, very tardily for your 2 dear letters, the last of the 12th Aug: when these dreadful news about your dear Mother-in-law[3] arrived, wh. distress me so very much. And how

[1] Ernie was a man of twenty-seven years.

[2] After leaving Bulgaria and marrying Johanna Loisinger, Prince Alexander had been created Count Hartenau. He died of peritonitis following an appendectomy in November 1893.

[3] Louis's mother, Princess of Battenberg, formerly Countess Julie Hauke. She was mortally ill and in fact died on the day this letter was written.

terrible for your dear Ludwig who is so devoted to his Mother & is so far away.[1] Could he come? I feel so much for him.

Beatrice came back so happy & Liko too having enjoyed her stay at Jugenheim & [Seeheim ?] so much. And now this terrible event is too sad! Of course they are ready to start at any moment. –

I was very glad that you were all together but dear Alicky on the dear 12th –

I cannot write abt. anything more now, but that we are all well –

Georgie & May & their big fine Boy[2] were here from the 3rd. Georgie is absent for a few days at Mar;[3] & we had a very pleasant visit of dear old Uncle Arthur M.[4] who left on Monday.

Hoping & praying for better news.

Ever your devoted Grandmama

V.R.I.

I miss my good faithful Francis C.[5] so much! Alas! we seem never to be out of sorrow & trouble. Kisses to the Children.

BALMORAL CASTLE

Oct 18th 1895

Darling Victoria,

I am anxious that these lines should reach you before you leave for Malta where I fear you may be left some time alone as the East is in such a disturbed state that Ludwig may be detained at some place or other. I trust not for long. He wrote me a most touching letter showing how intense his grief for his dear Mother's loss was! She was so proud of him & loved him so much. I will write to thank him soon. – Let me thank you for your dear letter of the 25th Sept. written soon after [the] sad loss of your dear kind Mother-in-law whom all her Children deeply mourn, including Auntie B. who was devoted to her. Poor little Alice too, it is touching to hear of her sorrow. I hope this feeling of affection & gratitude will always be encouraged as her dear Grandmama was so fond of & kind to her. – She was much beloved at Jugenheim & Darmstadt, was so charitable & kind to all the poor etc. You will I am sure try to make them feel that you will follow her example, & pray also do not neglect going to Church there, even if the Services may not always

---

[1] Louis was serving in the Mediterranean, commanding H.M.S. *Cambrian*.

[2] David, later Prince of Wales, King Edward VIII and Duke of Windsor.

[3] Home of Louise, eldest daughter of the Prince and Princess of Wales, who married the Earl (later Duke) of Fife.

[4] A cousin of the Queen's, Count Arthur Mensdorff-Pouilly.

[5] Her Highland Attendant, Francis Clark, who died 7 July 1895.

# Heiligenberg

Beatrice. July 29th – Aug 4th 1894.
29ten Juli — 4. Aug. 1894 Liko –

Ethel Cadogan    Aug. 11th & 14th 1894

Dudley    Sept. 5 – 12  1894

Ernie.    "    "    "

Alice    "    "    "

Wember    "    "    "

C. Schneider    "    "    "

Christian Victor of Sch Holstein    Sept 10 — 12  1894

Frangois    in Sept — —  1894

Thekla von Rauschen    4 Juni – 18 Juli 1895

Ernie.    16th July — 18th — 1895.

Augohskine Wengsl    "    "

be the best. For the setting of the people a good example is so necessary.

We have had a fine autumn. The time for darling Alix's[1] confinement is getting very near, & I feel very anxious all shld go off well. I dread that Russian Doctor!

How unfortunate that Ducky shld have sprained her ankle just now when she wld have liked to be at Coburg.

We have had a great deal of fine weather.

I must end with every good wish for you all & the darling Children – Auntie Beatrice says Georgie[2] is a splendid & delightful Boy.

Ever your devoted Grandmama

V.R.I.

WINDSOR CASTLE

[December 8th 1895]

Darling Victoria,

How wrong it is not to have written before this, but my overwhelming work & correspondence & my weak sight – make it very difficult [to] write. I think of you & the dear little Trio all the same & very very often. I am so grieved to think of you all alone at Malta never having seen dear Ludwig at all! & I am afraid affairs are so bad in Asia Minor that he may have to remain away! It would have been better if you had remained at Darmstadt.

You will now see dear Irène & Henry & Ella & Ernie & Ducky will have written to you & all about darling Alicky who is entirely wrapt up in her splendid Baby.

Dear Liko sailed[3] at 5 this mng. It is a great anxiety to me, but a very gallant thing for him to do wh. is much appreciated. But the parting on Tuesday was very sad when they went to Bagshot for the night. Yesterday mng. poor dear Auntie went with him to Aldershot & saw him start with all the other Officers & Men – very moving – but she is so good, so brave & unselfish – it is wonderful. She [was] back at 2 yesterday.

The weather has been vy. cold untill [*sic*] today, it blew a fearful gale for 3 days. I will write to Ludwig for Xmas & New Year. We are very pleased to have Franzjos[4] with us for Xmas & New Year.

[1] Grand Duchess Olga, the first of Alicky's and Nicky's girls, was born 15 November 1895.

[2] Victoria's first son.

[3] Weary of an inactive life, and determined to sustain the Hessian tradition of military prowess, Prince Henry had persuaded the Queen to let him volunteer for the Ashanti (Gold Coast) campaign.

[4] Prince Louis's younger brother Prince Francis Joseph was still unmarried. He married Anna, Princess of Montenegro, in 1897.

Poor Darmstadt must be very lonely without your dear Mother-in-law & Marie. Poor Ernie & Ducky must be terribly alone. They are now at Tsarkoe Selo.[1] What do you say to Sandra's[2] & Maud's engagements? Sandra is again too young.

Goodbye & God bless you.

Ever your devoted Grandmama

V.R.I.

In the ten years since he had been living in the Royal household, for nearly all the time close to the Queen, Prince Henry of Battenberg had provided a wise and reassuring masculine presence. Queen Victoria referred to him as her 'ray of light' in a world that had been mostly dark and anxious since the death of her own wise counsellor, friend and husband. She had yielded reluctantly to Liko's plea to go military campaigning, and one senses yet again that her prophetic vision played a part in her first decision to refuse permission.

Prince Henry went off with a high heart, and the Queen and Princess Beatrice heard on Christmas Day that he had reached Cape Coast Castle and that his regiment would soon be marching inland. Alas! poor Liko almost at once contracted malaria and had to be sent home. He died at sea before his ship reached England.

WINDSOR CASTLE

Feb 22 1896

Darling Victoria,

You have I am sure forgiven my not answering before – or thanking you for your 2 [letters] recd on the 12th 31st Jany.

I have been overwhelmed with writing & can no longer write as much as formerly as I have difficulty in *reading* what I have written. But I know dear Ludwig will have told *you all*, our utter misery – the impressive & heartrending ceremonies of the 4th & 5th – how wonderfully & admirably darling Auntie behaved & behaves! But how *too, too* dreadful it all is!

[1] The Russian palace complex outside St Petersburg.

[2] Princess Alexandra of Saxe-Coburg-Gotha (formerly Edinburgh) became engaged to Prince Ernest of Hohenlohe-Langenburg three months earlier. She was only seventeen. The Queen writes 'again' because her two elder sisters also became engaged 'too young'.

The sunbeam in our Home is *gone*! It breaks my heart to think of darling Auntie & her darling Children. Ludwig was so kind & affte to her & to poor dear little Drino – & Franzjos too – their grief was so affecting. I have good accounts from Auntie – her health is good & the bright sunshine & beautiful Country soothes her – The sympathy in the Country & appreciation of darling Liko who was universally beloved is unequalled. Everyone in mourning. All so kind.

I can hardly bear associating (excepting for business) with those who were not with me at that terrible time, & to hear Georgie's little boy[1] call him 'Papa' & to think of our poor little darlings who can no longer do so, was terribly upsetting. –

Did Ludwig get a Photograph of the Church & little Chapel & of the ship? If not I will send them to him.

Ever your devoted Mama [*sic*]<br>V.R.I.

I rejoice to think I shall see you D.V. dearest Victoria.

WINDSOR CASTLE

May 6 1896

Darling Victoria,

Many loving thanks for last dear letter of the [blank] – We were very sorry to leave the beautiful Riviera with the deep blue sky & sea & the lovely flowers & balmy air – but we find sunshine here, everything very green & the laburnum out. – after a good jny.

But oh! the return [and] the missing [of] our beloved Liko at every turn. His empty room & all his things *quite* overwhelmed darling Auntie, who is good, so brave and unmurmuring & resigned – that one can but admire her & wish to do everything in the world to save her every additional trouble & worry & lessen her bitter anguish.

Tell dear Ludwig that the Blonde[2] will within a few weeks be transferred to the Cape Station. He & Capt. Pöe are to get the 4th Class of the new Order[3] at once.

We are so sorry for good dear Mr. Sahl[4] such a good, attentive old friend.

I shall send by next Messenger my letter for Nicky & my birthday gift for dear Ludwig.

[1] The future Edward VIII and Duke of Windsor.
[2] The body of Prince Henry was brought to Madeira in H.M.S. *Blonde*, the journey being completed in H.M.S. *Blenheim*.
[3] The Victorian Order had just been instituted.
[4] Hermann Sahl, the Queen's German librarian, who died in May 1896.

I must end now. Do write & tell me something about Moscow & ask Ludwig to write. –

Ever your devoted Grandmama<br>V.R.I.

I am very pleased at the news[1] about Irène.


BALMORAL CASTLE

June 1 1896

Darling Victoria,

How dear & kind to write to me such a long & interesting letter about the Coronation & telling me just all I wished to know. The best description or at least the best written is in the D. Telegraph by Sir E. Arnold who wrote the Light of Asia. –

But oh! how awful & dreadful is that fearful catastrophe of that Fête![2] It is simply ghastly. – Would it not have been better to have stopped the Balls etc. for it looks so unfeeling to go on just the same. It must throw such a gloom over everything & I fear will distress Serge & Ella very much.

Will you be able to come to England with Ludwig? It wld be *so* nice. I send you a snd [signed] photograph you may like to have, just taken.

Who has Alicky got as Nurse? I fear if the nurse does not understand that Orchie[3] is responsible [and she is] under her, that it will never work.

I must end for today.

Ever your devoted Grandmama<br>V.R.I.

Alicky is not again expecting a Baby as the papers hint at?[4]
Thank dear Ludwig for his kind letter recd. this mng.


[1] She was soon to give birth to her second son, Prince Sigismund.

[2] At the Russian coronation (Nicky and Alicky had been married eighteen months and the first child had already been born), gifts were to be distributed to the people on the Hodynka, a large stretch of open ground outside Moscow. Some 700,000 turned up, there was a panic, and in the crush about 1,300 were killed or wounded.

[3] Mrs Mary Anne Orchard, recently nurse to the Hessian children. She had agreed to help Alicky with her children and live at the Russian court.

[4] Not yet. Grand Duchess Tatiana, the second daughter, was born twelve months later.

Aug 26 1896
Dear Gdpap's anniversary

Darling Victoria,

I must thank you for your last dear letter of the 24th July. Every thing went off so well at *Moscow* except that dreadful Catastrophe wh. cast a gloom over everything! – You may imagine my joy at seeing my darling Alicky again after now more than 2 years & after all she has erlebt.[1]

But now I am most anxious that Ella & Serge shld. pay us a little visit after Alicky & Nicky have been with us – or before – if only for a week or 10 days. I long so to see them & it *wld.* do poor dear Auntie good. She is so fond of [you] all & I have not seen Serge for 2 years & ½ Do try if it cannot be arranged.

Is it true that Serge was much hurt at the Ukase[2] abt. the accident & considered that it reflected on him?

The contrast here [illegible] happy year & many happy years especially 85 & 86 & the blank, the longing the missing our darling Liko are all more & more felt. I feel quite lost. But she is well in health & so good, & patient & resigned – so brave. But the thought that it must go on, so for ever on Earth – are [*sic*] terrible. It is too too terrible for me too.

We dread Balmoral beyond measure, but Alicky's visit & also Franzjos' [will do] her good. The leaving the beloved sweet Resting place will be a great wrench. – It is so peaceful there & will be so pretty.

You must be feeling very lonely & sad at Jugenheim – where all is so silent & sad now. All gone & dear Ludwig absent. Will you sisters all be at Darmstadt to receive dear Alicky.

Hoping to hear soon from you
Ever your devoted Grandmama
V.R.I.

How is dear little Alice getting on & dear little Louise & Georgie. I send you a new photograph of me & little Edward of York.

I am so glad that you found Irène well – & that you like their new property.[3]

---

[1] Gone through.
[2] Government edict. Serge was Governor-General of Moscow.
[3] Hemmelmark, near Kiel in north Germany.

BALMORAL CASTLE
                                                    Oct 21 1896
Darling Victoria,

I was just going to write to you to thank you for your dear letter of the 18th when I recd. your of the — for which many thanks.

Your account of Ducky gave me great pleasure & I am sure she will become of more & more use to Ernie & she shld be able to hold her own to be able to be of use to him. I hope there will be another Baby – a Son, let us hope. Is there *nothing* coming?

*22nd* I could not finish this yesterday & do so today. Do tell me, was there any truth in the story in all the papers that Nicky was unwell at the Elysée after the dinner? I am most anxious to hear from him as matters in Turkey[1] are threatening more & more, & there is the greatest danger of fresh massacres – wh. really are too dreadful. –

Is not Baby Olga[2] too delicious? She is one of the most charming Babies I ever saw. Who have you got as Governess for your dear little Alice & Louise?

The new Admiral Sir J. Hopkins[3] – told me he wld. certainly send Ludwig to the Riviera[4] if D.V. we go there. – I dread to look forward when we think of this dreadful January & Feb. I dread the return to Windsor for darling Auntie so much – every day will become an anniversary!

Do let me hear from you again before you leave. We shall probably stop here till the 12th or 13th Nov. –

I must end for today.

                                        Ever your devoted Grandmama
                                                    V.R.I.


EXCELSIOR HOTEL REGINA, CIMIEZ
                                                    Ap 21 1897
Darling Victoria,

I must write to you to tell you how often you are in my thoughts! Today I talked to Thora of your charming stay. Yesterday too I drove on the corniche some way further than we did that day fortnight (your

---

[1] The Turkish Empire was beset by nationalist uprisings, and counter-measures, like the Armenian massacres, gave great concern, especially in Britain.

[2] Grand Duchess Olga, Alicky's baby.

[3] C.-in-C. Mediterranean Fleet.

[4] When the Queen wintered in the south of France, the Mediterranean Fleet provided a 'guard ship', which anchored close by, but more as a courtesy to the monarch than as protection.

birthday) & drove back by the route[1] wh is beautiful. But there were clouds – & the distance was not so clear as the fortnight before –

21st Since I began this letter in wh I was so much interrupted I got your dear letter of the 16th, & quite understand Alix's reasons, wh I shall tell Lady Ampthill.[2]

This war between Greece & Turkey is too dreadful & makes me very unhappy. Poor Aunts Vicky & Alix are quite distracted.

But I am sure it will have to be stopped. – But Germany or rather William behaves too shamefully.

I saw today the other bride Dora of Coburg[3] who is not 16 till the end of the month. Ernst Günther is delighted but the marriage is not to be till she is 17.

Poor Anastasie[4] is in the greatest distress. – Aunt Beatrice went at once to see her. The end was too sad.

I am sure you will be sorry to leave Malta not knowing when you see it again! –

We are very very sorry to have to leave this day week. We are all unberufen well & the stay here has done me great good.

Your devoted Mama [*sic*]

V.R.I.

I send you 4 Photographs of my room, the Dining room, Drwg room & Chapel.

WINDSOR CASTLE

Nov 17 1897

Darling Victoria,

I was so glad to get your dear letter as I had not heard from you for so long. The visit of Alicky & Nicky for a whole month must have been a great pleasure to you all. I hear Alicky is grown very large. Does she still go on nursing.[5] I think it a great mistake in her position.

You mourn dear Aunt Mary Teck[6] with us, as I was sure you wld.

---

[1] There is an illegible word here. 'Coast'? The Queen's handwriting becomes increasingly difficult to decipher as she approaches the end of her life.

[2] Lady-of-the-Bedchamber.

[3] Princess Dorothea of Saxe-Coburg-Gotha. She married the Duke of Schleswig-Holstein on 2 August 1898.

[4] Grand Duchess Anastasia Michailovna of Russia. Her husband, Frederick Francis III of Mecklenburg-Schwerin had died on 10 April.

[5] The Queen had a lifelong aversion to mothers feeding their own children, and was shocked when some of her own daughters and grand-daughters insisted on doing so.

[6] The future Queen Mary's mother, grand-daughter of King George III, died 27 October 1897.

She was a true, warm friend & so clever & charming. Dear Mama was a very great friend of hers. Poor Uncle Teck is in a most sad & anxious state which is a terrible trouble to the poor sons & dear good May. It was so terribly sudden, but she had been very imprudent. –

You will have seen dear Sandra & Ernie[1] who spent 3 very pleasant weeks with us at Balmoral. They are so happy together.

We thought Franzjos & Anna had gone to Russia. Is she quite well? I suppose there are no *prospects*? What has been the matter with them? –

I am so glad that Nona Kerr[2] answers so well. – Poor dear Ella's having the measles is annoying – but Serge telegraphs that she is doing very well. –

We shall be delighted to see you in January. Christmas is a time I dread now & the days are coming wh. bring back all the anguish & *hopes* of 2 years ago! officers going to Africa & the terrible War going on in the Frontier of India bring all so home to us. Poor Col. McBean[3] has lost a son who was in that heroic Regt. of Gordon Highlanders. It is very sad.

We had a beautiful autumn at dear Balmoral & it was so warm.


EXCELSIOR HOTEL REGINA, CIMIEZ

April 1 1898

Darling Victoria,

I have not yet thanked you for your dear letter of 25 Feb – I hope you & the children are well & that Ludwig has kept quite well & had no return of gout. Being here reminds me so much of you & last year. But we are not so fortunate in the weather at least not for the last week when it blew & was very cold & on Sunday & Thursday (yesterday) it poured & we have [*sic*] had at least 3 times thunder & lightning at night & in the [illegible] & [illegible] this mng – & we never had any in the preceding years.

Poor Uncle Affie[4] has been very ill. He was very alarmingly so in

[1] Ernest, Hereditary Prince of Hohenlohe-Langenburg and his wife, Princess Alexandra, daughter of Affie and Marie, now Duke and Duchess of Saxe-Coburg-Gotha.

[2] Miss Kerr had just taken over as Lady-in-Waiting to Victoria, with special responsibility for helping to teach the children.

[3] One of the Queen's Serjeants-at-Arms. His son had probably been killed in the Indian Frontier uprising.

[4] *En route* to Malta, the Duke had suffered from a mosquito bite which went septic. There is no known clue to the identity of his 'old trouble'. He died two years later of cancer of the throat. The Queen, eighty-one years old then, was suffering one of her periods of 'black death'. 'Oh, God! my poor darling Affie gone too . . .' she exclaimed.

For H.G.D.H. Princess Louis of Battenberg.

Osborne.

Dinner List.

Saturday:- 12th February 1898

1        The Queen.

1  H.R.H.Princess Henry of Battenberg.

1  H.G.D.H.Princess Louis of Battenberg.

1  The Countess of Lytton.

1  The Hon'ble Aline Majendie.

1  Miss Nona Kerr.

1  Major the Hon'ble E.Noel. Rifle Brigade.

1  Colonel Cradock,5th Vol:Batt:Hampshire Regt.

1  Lieut Colonel Sir Arthur Bigge.

1  Major the Hon'ble H.C.Legge.

1  The Master of the Household.

11.

going fr. Alexandria to Malta and had to remain there seven [?] days. This voyage to Sicily & Nice did him great good but unfortunately his old [?] trouble he had suffered from 15 years ago (one like little Louise Fife had) shewed itself & developped [*sic*] vy rapidly after he reached Villefranche on the 23rd & necessitated a very severe but successful operation on the 26th wh. however has succeeded perfectly & he is doing well, but quite confined to bed & will be for at least another week.

2nd. – I was able to visit dear Uncle Affie, the 'Surprise' having been brought into the Inner [?] Harbour on Thursday mg & yesterday afternoon I was *rolled* from the Quay over a gangway & went on board & went quite easily on [into] Uncle Affie's Cabin. He is still quite bed [ridden] where he must remain for another week.

I have seen that poor unfortunate girl.[1] It is most awfully [illegible] & a ghastly story. She was perfectly unconscious not shy or put out, they say never seemed to *know any*thing & [4 words illegible] had had a child even. Her Parents have [?] through their stupid behaviour made the thing so public & the Anhalts also have been very unkind.

Augusta Strelitz[2] has been most kind but I think she shld [?] keep her a little now out of sight as I fear it is much talked of.

3rd. – I find that this letter wld reach you on your dear birthday wh. you spent with us last year, so I add my warmest & most affte. wishes for many many happy returns of that dear day wh. you spent with us last year here!

God bless you. We are so happy to have Marie Erbach[3] here. Gusta left today and he really was not so deaf.

Ever your devoted Grandmama<br>V.R.I.

BALMORAL CASTLE

Nov 8 1898

Darling Victoria,

I have to thank you for 2 dear letters of the 9 Sep & 23 Oct wh. I know you will have excused my not answering be not answer as I wished [before as I wished]. I was so sorry not to see you while you & the Children & dear Ludwig were in England. But I am much grieved about dear little Louise.[4] She certainly walked badly & the dear Child seemd always rather delicate. I hope the *cure* wh. seems a good thing, will prove successful & that the dear Children will both thrive, *well*.

I can't help feeling a little anxious about dear Irène's long journey & especially regret that the Seckendorffs[5] don't go with her. He wld have been invaluable being travelled so much himself. –

We have had a beautiful autumn, so little frost that the leaves are on

[1] Duchess Marie of Mecklenburg-Strelitz, grand-daughter of the Queen's cousin, Princess Augusta, had been seduced by a footman and had given illegitimate birth. Ostracised by her parents, her grandmother had taken her to the south of France. Here, the future Queen Mary joined them and advised them to tell the full and unexpurgated story to the Queen.

[2] Grand Duchess of Mecklenburg-Strelitz.

[3] Louis of Battenberg's sister Marie, Princess of Erbach-Schönberg.

[4] She was suffering from mild curvature of the spine, which soon cured itself. But the shadow of haemophilia was ever-present in the minds of the Queen and the girl's mother.

[5] Count Seckendorff, tutor to Prince Henry of Prussia, and now Maréchal de la Cour to Prince Henry's family, or Comptroller of the Household.

most of the trees & the colours are beautiful. – For the last month we have [had] a good deal of rain, but not more than one or two really wet days – & generally sunshine in the mng or else afternoon. –

The prospect of seeing dear Ella on the 12th when we hope to reach Windsor, is an immense pleasure as we see her so seldom. Aunt Vicky came here on the 1st Oct. with young Vicky & Adolph who left again on the 22nd & Aunt Vicky herself left on the 31st to pay some visits & meets us at Windsor on the Nov. 12th.

Dear Auntie Beatrice is unberufen much better for Kissingen. She photographs a great deal & most successfully. I send you 2 of me (groups with the York children [&] with Uncle Bertie little Edward & Victoria of Wales).

I hope Ducky & Ernie are both well?

Thank God! the Fashoda affair[1] has ended peaceably. To fight about such a thing wld have been dreadful, & to fight at all too awful!

Give my love to Alice & believe me always,

Your devoted old Grandmama<br>V.R.I.

When does Alicky come back from [indecipherable] Poor Aunt Alix feels her Mother's[2] death deeply. She returned last Tuesday.

OSBORNE

Dec 21 1898

Darling Victoria,

I thank you very much for your dear letter of the 11th.

How anxious you must have been about poor dear Toddy[3] but you must have been a great comfort to the poor Seckendorffs, the Tutor & good Millington[4] to have you [*sic*] Now you have the great pleasure of having Ludwig with you & looking particularly well I thought. But it will not be long. Only, of course if the poor Admiral had not had to give up – he wld. have just the same had to go on leaving you. I am delighted to see you again & the dear Children.

I hope dear little Louise is recovering & is much better.

I heard Ernie & dear Ducky are also well. But from all sides I hear

---

[1] A political crisis with France which nearly ended in war. It originated in the disputed possession of an area of the Sudan.

[2] The Princess of Wales's mother was Louise, Princess of Hesse, wife of Prince Christian of Schleswig-Holstein, who became King of Denmark in 1863.

[3] Prince Waldemar of Prussia, Princess Irène's son.

[4] Nurse to the above.

bad accounts of Alfred who has been ruining his health & looks dreadfully ill.

Potsdam has been morally & physically most injurious to him, it is
*most* grievous for he is the only son!

These last 4 days have been beautiful & bright.

Hoping that Franzjos & Anna are well,

Ever your devoted Grandmama<br>V.R.I.

I wish you all a very happy Christmas.


EXCELSIOR HOTEL REGINA, CIMIEZ
April 1 1899

Darling Victoria,

It is so very long since I wrote to you, but I was much pleased to get
your kind letter & am very grateful for it.

Poor Aunt Marie & Uncle Alfred's wishes about young Arthur, I
fear are an impossibility wh. Ernie will be able to tell you. The whole
family is united in thinking it must be Charlie. But Uncle A. has got [it]
into his head it must be young Arthur[1] I will not here dwell on the
almost if not *quite* insuperable difficulties of that & all the advantages of
the other arrangement. – 3rd. I go on today & wish you all possible
happiness & many returns of your dear birthday wh. you spent here, 2
years ago. I am so sorry that you will again be separated from dear
Ludwig[2] who will, I fear not be back even for his own birthday.

My present is what you wished – a Chair.

We have had the whole family here. Dear May who came out with us,
left this mng. to our great regret, for she is so dear & und passt so gut
zu uns.[3]

Uncle Bertie & Aunt Louise[4] are still at Cannes tho' the latter leaves

[1] Affie's only son Prince Alfred of Great Britain and Hereditary Prince of
Saxe-Coburg-Gotha, had died of tuberculosis unmarried and before he could
succeed to the title. The succession was therefore in doubt. Charlie is Charles
Edward, Duke of Albany on the death of his haemophilic father, Prince
Leopold. Young Arthur is the son of Prince Arthur of Connaught, son of
the Duke, who married Alexandra, Duchess of Fife in her own right.

[2] Louis was Flag-Captain of H.M.S. *Majestic*, flagship of the Channel Fleet.
He took up a home shore appointment as Assistant Director of Naval Intelligence in June.

[3] Fits in so well.

[4] Queen Victoria's fourth daughter became Duchess of Argyll on her husband's succession the following year.

tomorrow. Aunt Vicky leaves Bordighera tomorrow. Uncle Affie was here for 10 days a fortnight ago – & Uncle Arthur & Aunt Louischen coming from Egypt were here for 6 days at the same time.

The 1st week was very fine & very warm – this followed a week with very cold wind tho' it was bright & this last week has been much warmer & finer. Yesterday was quite splendid & all the flowers are coming out.

Aunt Lenchen came on the 29th & Thora[1] also came out with us & as well as little Leop[d].[2] Ena & Maurice[3] have remained behind. – And good bye & God bless you.

Ever your devoted Grandmama

V.R.I.

Kisses to the dear trio.

Although a grief to her, the Boer War of 1899 also acted as a great emotional and physical spur to the weakening Queen. She did everything within her failing powers to add strength and encouragement to the British cause. She inspected departing troops by the thousand, even if she could not always descend from her carriage and, with her poor sight, could scarcely see them – though she could distinguish khaki ('very practical') from the more colourful uniforms of the Highland Regiments. 'May God protect you!' she told her soldiers time and again, and everywhere they cheered her, and 'I went home with a lump in my throat'.

BALMORAL CASTLE

Nov 7 1899

Darling Victoria,

I have not answered your last dear letter from London but do so now. From Franzjos and Anna you will have heard of all our doings this Autumn. We are entirely absorbed in the War which causes me such anxiety & while I [several words illegible] Soldiers & also of the most efficient [?] help of the Naval Brigade the other day over Ladysmith, my hearts bleeds most truly and deeply for the many losses we have sustained & for the sorrow of so many many families high and low! – I

---

[1] 'Aunt Lenchen's' daughter, Helena Victoria called 'Thora'. She did not marry.

[2] Prince Leopold, son of Princess Henry (Beatrice) of Battenberg.

[3] Prince Maurice of Battenberg.

assure you it makes me quite miserable. Since I began this, good news
of a successful action & advance [?] have come [?] saying Boers were
driven a good way back & 2 guns taken & Ladysmith quite safe. Ludwig will have heard all this. I long to see you both.

Since 4 days we have very bad weather again & the most changeable
but not cold. Very little frost. I hope the dear children are well. We
leave on Friday.

Ever Your devoted Grandmama,<br>
V.R.I.

Forgive my untidy writing but I was in such a hurry & so often interrupted.


No greater sacrifice was made by the Queen than her decision to
forgo her usual holiday in the south of France – or some other
warm place – during the worst months of the winter. Instead, she
decided to visit Ireland, as a gesture of encouragement to the
people and of gratitude for the part Irish soldiers were playing in
the war in South Africa. The sacrifice was made heavier by the
fact that she had for long been exasperated and wearied by the
restlessness and political disaffection of her Irish subjects. It was
nearly forty years since she had visited Ireland, and she had always refused to set up an establishment there.

'Her reception was all that could be wished, and it vindicated
her renewed confidence in the loyalty of the Irish people to the
Crown, despite the continuance of political agitation. The days
were spent busily and passed quickly. She entertained the leaders
of Irish society, attended a military review and an assembly of
52,000 schoolchildren in Phoenix Park and frequently drove
through Dublin and the neighbouring country.' – *Queen Victoria:
a Biography* (1902) by Sidney Lee.


VICE REGAL LODGE, PHOENIX PARK, DUBLIN
April 4 1900

Darling Victoria,

Let me wish you many, many happy returns of your dear birthday on
which I wish I could have [?] seen you. May God bless and protect you.
My gift or *one* of them is a Cloak I heard you wished for & I shall get
you something nice from here.

The weather had changed when we got to Holyhead. We started at
once & had a very fair passage, quite smooth for the first three hours –

and the last a little rough – The dear old yacht went beautifully. We
Land [*sic*] 11.30 & met with a most enthusiastic Reception from thou-
sands & thou[sands] in Dublin & the Town was beautifully decorated.
The drive from Kingstown here took 2 hours & a ½!
    With love to Ludwig & the dear children
                                Ever your devoted old Grandmama,
                                                            V.R.I.


                              BALMORAL
                                                        June 10 1900
Darling Victoria,
    I have not written to you about the disappointment at Darmstadt. I
hope however that as she is so much stronger we shall have another
Event before too long which will repair this blow![1]
    I thank you so much for your dear letter for my birthday and your
pretty & useful Covers. Auntie B. has been enjoying her tour favoured
by beautiful weather. She sailed for the Scilly Islands today. We have
had bright weather but cold – then very hot and from the 2nd till the
6th when we had thunder (distant) which brought rain and chilliness
till today when it was very warm again. Georgie left us yest'day but
dear May and the children remain with us till next Saturday.
    We breakfast in the Cottage for the 1st time today but I have been
sitting there for some days.
    I hope you are not feeling too uncomfortable[2] and that we may be in
time to be of use. When does Mrs Paterson come? Don't put her off too
long. I am very anxious and hope that the expected little one may bear
my name of whatever sex it may be – as it will be born where your
dear Gt GdMama lived and under the shadow as it were of the Castle.
    We had a nice visit from the present Sirdar Sir R. Wyngate [*sic*]. I
trust the dear Children are well. With love to Ludwig.
                                Ever your devoted GdMama
                                                            V.R.I.
The news of the War which people were so wild about after the Capture

    [1] The blow refers to a miscarriage or still-birth suffered by Ducky, Grand
Duchess of Hesse. It was probably not the only one in her brief first marriage
for she was wild in her ways and rode hard even when pregnant. This mishap
may have hastened the end of the marriage which ended in divorce on 21
December 1901 – mercifully after the death of the Queen. They both re-
married happily, Ducky to Grand Duke Cyril of Russia, and Ernie to Eleonore, Princess of Solms-Hohensolms-Lich, by whom he had two sons.
    [2] Victoria was with child. Prince Louis ('Dickie') was born 25 June 1900.
The old Queen was godmother to the future Earl Mountbatten of Burma.

of Pretoria are not so good excepting for Sir R. B. Buller which are very good.

WINDSOR CASTLE

July 13 1900

Darling Victoria,

I am so sorry I did not see you today to wish you many happy returns of dear little Louise's birthday! I hope you have not suffered from the great heat which has made me fit for nothing.

There is one thing which would give me great pleasure if you and Ludwig approved of it, viz. if you would add the name Albert to the 4 others.

Ever your devoted Gd Mama<br>V.R.I.

It need hardly be added that Princess Victoria complied with Queen Victoria's request in the second paragraph of the above letter. The future Dickie Mountbatten, Admiral of the Fleet, created an Earl and Knight of the Garter, was christened Albert Victor Nicholas Louis Francis, though the names Louis and Francis were put first after the Queen died.

The aged, rheumatic Queen held the big baby all through the christening ceremony, when he showed early signs of boisterousness by knocking off her spectacles.

At this time, close to the end of the Queen's life (she died 22 January 1901), Prince Louis of Battenberg was one of her closest confidants, had been appointed Trustee of her private estate and Personal naval aide-de-camp.

As for Princess Victoria, her most remarkable quality is the strength and independence of her mind. From an early age she refused to be overwhelmed by her formidable grandmother. Nor was the Queen allowed to play any part in the choice of Victoria's own husband: the marriage was the only completely successful one in the Hessian family.

Princess Victoria remained a loving and intimate granddaughter to the end, when she was among those at Osborne when the Queen died.

# Name index

by Douglas Matthews